CONTRACT LAW IN ZAMBIA: AN INTRODUCTION

CONTRACT LAW IN ZAMBIA: AN INTRODUCTION

by

Sangwani Patrick Ng'ambi
LLB (De Montfort) LLM (Cornell) PhD (Leicester)

First Edition 2018

First Floor, Sunclare Building, 21 Dreyer Street, Claremont 7708

ISBN: 978 1 48512 757 4

Typeset in 12/14 Times New Roman
Typesetting by Helanna Typesetting

To Gail and JJ

ABOUT THE AUTHOR

Sangwani Patrick Ng'ambi holds a Bachelor of Laws degree from De Montfort University and a Master of Laws degree from Cornell University. In addition, he holds a Doctor of Philosophy degree from the University of Leicester, where he was a Commonwealth Scholar. He qualified as an Advocate of the High Court of Zambia in June 2017.

Dr Ng'ambi joined the University of Zambia's School of Law in October 2008. He specialises in International Investment Law, International Trade Law, Contracts and Torts. At present he also serves as Chief Editor of the Zambia Law Journal. Prior to this, he served as Assistant Dean (Undergraduate) and Assistant Dean (Research).

ABOUT THE COMMISSIONING AND SERIES EDITOR

Evance Kalula is Emeritus Professor of Law at the University of Cape Town. He recently retired as Director of the International Academic Programmes Office and the Confucius Institute. He has held a personal chair as professor of employment law and social security. He holds several degrees in law, including a PhD. He was educated at the University of Zambia School of Law; Kings College, London; Balliol College, Oxford (where he was a Rhodes scholar) and the University of Warwick School of Law. He specialises in international and comparative labour law, international trade, regional integration and social security. He previously served as Chair of the South African Employment Conditions Commission (ECC), member of the International Labour Organization (ILO) Commission of Inquiry on Freedom of Association in Zimbabwe and Chair of the University of Lusaka (UNILUS) Council. He is currently a member of the Ministerial Advisory Panel of the South African Economic Development Department (EDD), fellow of the African Academy of Sciences (AAS), advisor to the Council of the Academy of Sciences of South Africa (ASSAf) and member of the Board of Institute for African Alternatives (IFAA). He is also the immediate Past President of the International Labour and Employment Relations Association (ILERA).

EDITOR'S PREFACE

Contract Law in Zambia: An Introduction is the first accessible and most comprehensive text on contract law to date. Dr Sangwani Patrick Ng'ambi has covered all the relevant aspects of the law of contract in Zambia, in both statutory and common (case) law.

Comprising 11 chapters, the book deals with all the basic elements of contract, from agreement to performance and the other features in between. It thus focuses on a range of topics, including the theoretical aspects, offer and acceptance, consideration, the intention to create legal relations, the terms of a contract, misrepresentation, duress and undue influence, void and illegal contracts, the discharge of a contract, and remedies for breach of contract.

Like a number of other branches of Zambian law, the law of contract is derived from English law, particularly the common law. The author stays true to that heritage by highlighting the important case law and related developments. However, it is gratifying that the author has paid attention to the increasing number of cases decided by the Zambian courts, which 'domesticate' and build on English law, and therefore highlight the relevance of the local context and the changes evolving as a result of home-grown adjudication.

A wide range of readers will find this book useful. The book has been written mainly for law students, broadly defined. However, other interested readers, including legal practitioners, corporate professionals and those in related disciplines, will find this book to be an indispensable resource.

Evance Kalula
Commissioning and Series Editor
June 2018

CONTENTS

Chapter 8: MISTAKE

Chapter 9: VOID AND ILLEGAL CONTRACTS

Chapter 10: DISCHARGE OF CONTRACT

Chapter 11: REMEDIES FOR BREACH OF CONTRACT

Chapter 1

CONTRACT THEORY

Contracts are written or spoken agreements that are enforceable by law. The elements and formalities required for the formation of a contract are extensively covered in this book. However, the aim of this chapter is to discuss the various theories pertaining to why contracts are enforceable in the first place. This chapter looks at the classical doctrine of contract law and utilitarian theories.

The classical doctrine, also known as the will theory, espouses the view that contracts freely entered into by the parties should be honoured. The only option the State has, once it is established that the agreement was indeed freely entered into and that it does indeed conform to all the relevant formalities, is to uphold and enforce it.[1] This theory is essentially based on the liberal premise that the law should only intervene in the discourse of human relations to prevent harm from coming to the individual. This was a relatively axiomatic theory until it was challenged by the reliance theory in the late nineteenth century. It did re-emerge in the 1980s, but other theories that challenge the classical doctrine have also emerged since then.

Utilitarian theories espouse that the purpose of contract law is to advance the greatest good for the greatest number. The most well-known utilitarian theory of contract law is the 'efficient breach' theory. It espouses that the goal of contract law is to promote efficiency. The way this is done is by avoiding waste and encouraging wealth maximisation. The latter is translated in monetary terms. This theory endorses the view that contracts should only be upheld if it would be efficient to do so.

1 THE CLASSICAL DOCTRINE

The classical doctrine of contract law is premised on 'freedom of contract'.[2] This essentially entails that parties are free to enter into contracts, on terms freely determined by themselves.[3] Once it is established that the agreement was indeed freely entered into and that all the relevant

[1] Spencer Nathan Thal 'The inequality of bargaining power doctrine: The problem of defining contractual unfairness' (1988) 8 *Oxford Journal of Legal Studies* 17–33, 21.

[2] Charles Fried *Contract as Promise: A Theory of Contractual Obligation* (1981) 1–2.

[3] Daniel P O'Gorman 'Contract theory and some realism about employee covenant not to compete cases' (2012) 65 *SMUL Rev* 145–202, 165.

elements are present, the only option the State has is to uphold and enforce the contract.[4] The will theory, however, has a number of gaps and cannot on its own explain why contracts are enforced. One of the tenets of the will theory, for example, is that a party is bound by a contract because they have uttered a promise, and that once they have done so they are bound by it. This view is diametrically opposed to that of reliance theorists, who advance the view that a promisee is bound by a contract not because of words uttered, but rather because the other party has relied on it.[5] Another question that arises is whether morality is in and of itself an adequate explanation for why contacts are enforced. Could it be that a party is bound not because they are morally obliged but because they have consented to it?

1.1 The classical doctrine of contract law

The classical theory of contract was propounded in the nineteenth century.[6] The theory is encapsulated by the term 'freedom of contract'. This essentially advances the proposition that the parties to a contract have absolute freedom in determining the way in which their relationship is to be governed.[7] As a consequence, the parties to a contract are free to agree on whatever they wish, with minimal State interference.[8] Provided there is a 'meeting of minds', the State has no choice but to enforce and uphold the contract.[9]

This theory emerged at a time when liberalism generally dominated economic and political philosophy.[10] One of the central tenets of this philosophy is individual autonomy: that the individual has absolute autonomy to do whatever they wish. The only time the State could intervene is to prevent harm coming to others.[11] Thus, for example, under 'laissez-faire' economics, which emanates from liberal theory, it is argued that the market works better if the State simply allows events to take their course. This is so even where the economy is in a seemingly precarious

---

[4] Thal n 1.

[5] See generally Lon L Fuller and William R Perdue 'The reliance interest in contract damages' (1936) 46 *Yale LJ* 52–96.

[6] James Gordley 'The moral foundations of private law' (2002) 47 *AM Juris* 1–23, 16.

[7] Jill Poole *Textbook on Contract Law* 11 ed (2012) 5.

[8] Randy E Barnett 'A consent theory of contract' (1986) 86 *Colum L Rev* 269, 300, where he states: 'According to the classical view, the law of contract gives expression to and protects the will of the parties, for the will is something worthy of respect.'

[9] Thal n 1, 21.

[10] Michael Furmston *Cheshire, Fifoot and Firmston's Law of Contract* 16 ed (2012) 22–25.

[11] John Stuart Mill *On Liberty* (1974) 69.

position.[12] In the spirit of this philosophy, the classical doctrine postulates that the central tenet of the contract theory is that the party is an autonomous entity.[13] It is no surprise that the will theory emerged at this time. In fact, it has been dismissed by reliance theorists as simply a manifestation of the prevailing political and economic philosophies of the nineteenth century.[14]

1.2 The reliance theory: a shift from the classical doctrine

The classical doctrine did lose some traction in the late nineteenth century.[15] It was somewhat overtaken by the reliance theory, which adopted 'a more socializing, communitarian ethos'.[16] It was advanced that the classical doctrine simply perpetuated inequality because the degree of freedom exercised was largely contingent upon the 'natural aptitude, education or the possession of wealth'.[17] Moreover, the requirement that the State and judge should passively uphold contracts freely entered into simply stifled the active role they really should have been playing.[18] These criticisms necessitated the adoption of a philosophy that was independent of the tenets of free choice and individual responsibility.[19] Thus emerged the reliance theory.

Reliance theorists postulate that contractual obligation stems not from a promise uttered, but rather from another party's reliance on that promise.[20] If a promissor induces a promisee to rely on them, the former has an obligation to ensure that the latter is not made worse off by such reliance. Such reliance must be reasonably foreseeable or justifiable.[21] In this sense, it can be argued that there is a blurring of the line between contract law and tort law.[22] The response to this assertion is that this has always been the

---

[12] See generally Milton Friedman *Capitalism and Freedom* (1962); cf John M Keynes *The General Theory of Employment Interest and Money* (1936).

[13] Mill n 11.

[14] Patrick S Atiyah 'Contracts, promises and the law of obligations' (1978) 94 *Law Quarterly Review* 193–223, 199.

[15] Charles Fried '*Contract as Promise* thirty years on' (2012) 45 *Suffolk University Law Review* 961–978, 961.

[16] Ibid.

[17] See Patrick S Atiyah *The Rise and Fall of Freedom of Contract* (1979) 6 for a discussion on inequality and fairness; see also Thal n 1, 28–29.

[18] Atiyah n 14, 221; Grant Gilmore *The Death of Contract* (1974) 15; but cf Carolyn Edwards 'Freedom of contract and fundamental fairness for individual parties: The tug of war continues' (2009) 77 *UKMC L Rev* 647–696, 656.

[19] Atiyah n 17, 6.

[20] See generally Fuller and Perdue n 5; Atiyah n 17; Gilmore n 18.

[21] Barnett n 8, 274.

[22] Gilmore n 18, 72; Atiyah n 17, 1; Atiyah n 14, 221–223.

case historically, and that the distinction between contract law and tort law only really emerged in the nineteenth century, when the classical doctrine was introduced.[23]

One of the difficulties with the reliance theory, however, is that it is incongruous with various central features of contract law.[24]

First, the reliance theory is at variance with the formation rules required under contract law. In order to form a contract, there must be an offer and there must be acceptance of that offer. It is therefore evident that 'agreement' is the primary basis on which liability arises under contract law, not 'reliance'.[25]

Secondly, the actual content of the obligations arising out of a contract are very different to those supposed by reliance theorists.[26] Under contract law, the primary obligation is to do what one has promised to do. This can be contrasted with reliance theorists, who contend that the only obligation on the promissor, where they cannot do as they had promised, is to reimburse the promisee for reliance losses.[27] Thus, under the reliance theory, it would appear that the party has only breached their contract if it is shown that the duty to reimburse has not been performed. However, this is not the case in reality: when parties enter into an agreement, they are expecting each side to perform their contractual obligations, not to be paid. Therefore, it is clear that duty in reality lies in performance, and not in reimbursement as advanced by reliance theorists.

1.3 The re-emergence of the classical doctrine

The classical theory was resurrected by Fried in 1981, when it was re-established that contractual obligations were distinct from tortious ones.[28] Under his 'promise principle', Fried postulated that once the parties had entered into a contract, they were morally obliged to fulfil the terms of that contract.[29] The idea of a morally binding promise advances individual autonomy, because it gives the party the freedom to bind their future self in order to advance the interests of their present self.[30]

---

[23] Atiyah n 17; Gilmore n 18, 87.

[24] Steven A Smith *Contract Theory* (2004) 90.

[25] Ibid.

[26] Smith n 24, 91.

[27] Smith n 24, 91–92.

[28] See generally Fried n 2; Curtis Bridgeman and John CP Goldberg 'Do promises distinguish contract from tort?' 45 *Suffolk University Law Review* 873–895, 890.

[29] Fried n 2, 1.

[30] Fried n 2, 14; see also Jody S Kraus 'The correspondence of contract and promise' (2009) 7 *Columbia Law Rev* 1603–1649, 1619.

Liberalism formed an intrinsic part of this private law; this was evident from areas of law such as tort, where the rights of the individual were well recognised. The law of contracts is a means through which parties can dispose of the individual rights contained in other areas of law. It therefore follows that 'the regime of contract law . . . carries to its natural conclusion the liberal premise that individuals have rights' and that the 'will theory of contract, which sees contractual obligations as essentially self-imposed, is a fair implication of liberal individualism'.[31]

At the heart of contractual obligations is individual autonomy and trust.[32] Once a promissor has given another party grounds to expect a promised performance, they must keep such promise.[33] Failure to do so amounts to an abuse of confidence, which is tantamount to lying. When a promise elicits the trust of another person, it entails an element of vulnerability. By lying or breaking a promise, one abuses that trust.[34] Morality under this principle is not about what people believe or think: it is guided by the principle that the 'gratuitous infliction of pain is wrong'.[35] What is important is how people lead their lives and treat each other.[36] Although morality recognises that people have projects and goals, a penumbra of which will have an effect on other people, the pursuit of these goals should not deliberately harm other people. As succinctly put by Fried, morality condemns 'a way of life indifferent to the wellbeing of others, and even more strongly condemns pursuits that are constituted by the frustration, humiliation or destruction of others'.[37]

Morality, however, cannot adequately explain the rationale behind the enforcement of contracts.[38] Although morality explains what the promissor ought to do, it does not explain why the courts should enforce contracts.[39] In addition, ordinary promises are not inherently enforceable.[40] The

[31] Fried n 2, 2.
[32] Fried n 2, 16.
[33] Ibid.
[34] Ibid.
[35] Ibid.
[36] Charles Fried 'The convergence of contract and promise' (2007) 120 *Harvard Law Review Forum* 1–9, 2.
[37] Fried n 36, 3; see also Fried n 15, 977–978.
[38] Andrew S Gould 'A property theory of contract' (2009) 103 *Northwestern University Law Review* 1–62, 20.
[39] Ibid.
[40] See also Bridgeman and Goldberg n 28, 875.

promissory theory fails to make a distinction between ordinary promises and legally enforceable ones.[41]

Contracts are not binding because of morality: they are binding because the parties have consented to the obligations contained therein.[42] Contract law is based primarily on the alienation and transfer of rights. The law is supposed to protect against the wrongful interference with this process. However, in order to determine whether an obligation has been created, there must be an intention to be legally bound.[43] For this reason, it is advanced that a promise is not in itself an adequate means through which contractual obligations are created.[44] The promise is simply a manifestation of an intention to be legally bound.[45] The intention is what renders the contract binding, not morality.

The will theory itself may also be inconsistent with various aspects of contract law. For example, the doctrines of mistake, frustration and impossibility are not promissory based.[46] This criticism has been countered by the contention that the courts tend to deal with such cases by applying legal principles such as tort and restitution, which are extrinsic to contract law.[47]

What is not adequately addressed is the discrepancy between the promissory theory and doctrines such as consideration.[48] To address this, Fried simply dismisses the doctrine as 'artificial and unfortunate'.[49] He states that 'the doctrine of consideration offers no coherent alternative basis for the force of contracts, while still treating promise as necessary to it'.[50] He argues that consideration serves more as evidence that 'the promise was made to me, and that I desired the promise to be made'.[51]

There are also concerns that the promissory model of contract law is not consistent 'with the objective approach that common law adopts for

[41] Gould (n 38) notes: 'This is not an easy distinction to make on promise-based principles. Unfortunately, Fried's promissory theory does not adequately explain why a moral duty of the promisor should translate into a legal right held by the promisee. Invoking the convention of promising, even in conjunction with values of autonomy and trust, does not bridge this conceptual gap.'

[42] Barnett n 8; Randy E Barnett 'Consenting to form contracts' (2002) 71 *Fordham L Rev* 627–645.

[43] Barnett n 8, 304.

[44] Barnett n 8, 305.

[45] Ibid; see also Randy E Barnett 'Contract is not promise; contract is consent' (2012) 45 *Suffolk University Law Review* 1–21, 10.

[46] O'Gorman n 3, 168; see also Smith n 24, 65–66, who raises similar objections.

[47] Fried n 2, 25; he discusses this matter further on p 60.

[48] Smith n 24, 65.

[49] Fried n 2, 25.

[50] Fried n 2, 37.

[51] Fried n 2, 42.

determining the existence and content of contractual obligations'.[52] The difficulty with this approach is that it focuses more on what the parties outwardly appear to intend to agree to than on what they actually intend to agree to.[53] This approach is also inconsistent with simultaneous transactions. An example of this is when a member of the public makes a purchase from a vending machine. In such instances, there is nothing 'resembling a promise or an agreement'; instead, the purchasing party is simply required to 'do something', such as inserting money into the vending machine. Yet these transactions in essence still constitute contracts. Furthermore, contracts are bilateral, whereas a promise is in essence a unitary act.

2 UTILITARIAN JUSTIFICATION: THE EFFICIENT BREACH THEORY

Utilitarian theories of contract law espouse the view that the law exists to promote the greatest good for the greatest number.[54] Although there are various utilitarian theories of contract law, the best known is the 'efficient breach' theory. Under the efficient breach theory, 'a party should be allowed to breach a contract and pay damages, if doing so would be more economically efficient than performing under the contract'.[55] One of the central tenets of the efficient breach theory is wealth maximisation, which is quantified monetary terms.[56]

The term 'efficiency' is seen through the prism of Pareto efficiency.[57] This is divided into two categories: Pareto optimality and Pareto superiority. Under Pareto optimality, behaviour is rendered efficient if one party's welfare is enhanced but at the expense of another.[58] Under Pareto

[52] Smith n 24, 60–61.

[53] Gilmore n 18, 41–45.

[54] See JH Burns and HLA Hart (eds) *The Collected Works of Jeremy Bentham* (1977) 393.

[55] Bryan A Garner (ed) *Black's Law Dictionary* (2009) 592.

[56] See Richard A Posner 'Utilitarianism, economics, and legal theory' (1979) 8 *J Legal Stud* 103, 119, who describes wealth maximisation thus: 'Wealth is the value in dollars or dollar equivalents (an important qualification, as we are about to see) of everything in society. It is measured by what people are willing to pay for something or, if they already own it, what they demand in money to give it up. The only kind of preference that counts in a system of wealth maximization is thus one that is backed up by money–in other words, that is registered in a market.'

[57] Contrast this with Kaldor–Hicks efficiency, under which it is argued that a rule is efficient if the benefits a party obtains from a rule are far greater than the losses incurred by those that might be harmed by it. See Richard S Markowitz 'Constructive critique of the traditional definition and use of the concept of the effect of a choice on allocative (economic) efficiency: Why the Kaldor–Hicks test, the Coase theorem, and virtually all law-and-economics welfare arguments are wrong' (1993) *U Ill L Rev* 485, 489.

[58] Jules L Coleman 'Efficiency, utility, and wealth maximization' (1980) 8 *Hofstra L Rev* 509, 512–513.

superiority, a rule is efficient if no person is made worse off by it, but at least one person benefits from it.[59] Pareto superiority is the utilised standard in defining efficiency according to the efficient breach theory.[60] This is because few people would object to policies that make at least one person better off while making no one else worse off.[61] Moreover, it has been observed that:

> Exchanges among knowledgeable, rational persons in a free market are generally Pareto superior; rational individuals do not strike bargains with one another unless each perceives it to be in his or her own interest to do so. A successful exchange between such parties is, therefore, one in which the value to each of what he or she relinquishes is perceived as less than the value of what each receives in return. Such exchanges make no individual worse off; often they improve the lot of all concerned. Pareto superiority is connected in this way to the ideal of a free-exchange market.[62]

As far as the remedies under contract law are concerned, it is advanced that the law promotes efficiency through its remedy of damages. This is accentuated by the fact that the dominant remedy under contract law is damages, not specific performance.[63] Once the promissor breaches an agreement, they are expected to pay damages as a remedy.[64] According to the efficient breach theory, there are instances where it might not be economically efficient to induce the promissor to complete performance of the contract.[65] An example of such a situation is given by Posner:

> Suppose I sign a contract to deliver 100 000 custom-ground widgets at 10¢ apiece to A for use in his boiler factory. After I have delivered 10 000, B comes to me, explains that he desperately needs 25 000 custom-ground widgets at once since otherwise he will be forced to close his pianola factory at great cost, and offers me 15¢ apiece for them. I sell him the widgets and as a result do not complete timely delivery to A, causing him to lose $1 000 in profits. Having obtained an additional profit of $1 250 on the sale to B, I am better off even after reimbursing A for his loss, and B is also better off. The breach is therefore Pareto superior. True had I refused to sell to B he could have gone to A and negotiated an assignment to him of part of A's contract to me. But this would have introduced an additional step, with additional transaction costs—and high ones, because it would be a bilateral monopoly negotiation.[66]

In such an instance, it would be efficient for the parties to repudiate the contract. This is provided that the promissor, who is able to profit from the

[59] Coleman n 58, 513.
[60] Coleman n 58, 520.
[61] Coleman n 58, 516.
[62] Coleman n 58, 516–517.
[63] Edwin Peel *Treitel on the Law of Contract* 13 ed (2011) 988, 1099.
[64] Robert Upex and Geoffrey Bennett *Davies on Contract* 10 ed (2008) 288–289; Oliver W Holmes *The Common Law* (1882) 300–301' Oliver Wendell Holmes 'The path of the law' (1897) 10 *Harv L Rev* 457.
[65] Richard A Posner *Economic Analysis of Law* 8 ed (2011) 150.
[66] Posner n 65, 151.

default, will place the promisee in as good a position as they would have been in had the performance been completed.[67] This means compensating the disappointed party not just for sunk costs but also for lost future profits. The object of contract law, in this respect, is to give the promissor an incentive to fulfil their contractual obligations, unless doing so would result in an inefficient use of resources.[68]

The efficient breach theory has been criticised as amounting to a 'prescriptive recommendation to act wrongfully'.[69] In addition, it is argued that it immorally enriches a party that breaches a contract.[70] The latter argument can be countered by the definition of morality espoused above. An act is only immortal if it is done without taking cognisance of the well-being and interests of others.[71] This is actually addressed by the fact that the disappointed promisee is paid damages, which includes lost future profits, from a particular transaction.[72] The payment of lost future profits not only restores the disappointed promisee to the position they would have been in had the breach not taken place, it also renders them indifferent to whether the contract is completed or not. It also gives the promissor an incentive to perform, unless breaching the contract will benefit them in some way, even after paying lost profits.[73] This way, one party makes a gain without the other parties losing out, which is certainly within the realm of Pareto superiority.

---

67 Robert Birmingham 'Breach of contract, damage measures, and economic efficiency' (1970) 24 *Rutgers L Rev* 273, 284.

68 Posner n 65, 150.

69 Seana V Shiffrin 'The divergence of contract and promise' (2007) 120 *Harv Law Rev* 708, 733.

70 See Daniel Friedman 'The efficient breach fallacy' (1989) 18 *J Leg Stud* 1; Shiffrin n 69; but cf Fried n 36, 5; Daniel Markovits and Alan Schwartz 'The myth of efficient breach: New defenses of the expectation interest' (2011) *Virginia L Rev* 1939, 1948; see also Avery Katz 'Virtue ethics and efficient breach' (2012) 45 *Suffolk University Law Review* 777–798, 784–785.

71 Fried n 36, 3.

72 Posner n 65, 150–151.

73 Ibid.

Chapter 2

OFFER AND ACCEPTANCE

To form a contract, four elements must be established: offer, acceptance, consideration and intention to be legally bound.[1] Without these elements, a contract is deemed unenforceable. Any potential plaintiff under an unenforceable contract is therefore left without a remedy under the contract in a court.[2] This chapter will look at offer and acceptance.

1 OFFER

An offer is 'an expression of willingness on the part of the offeror to contract with the offeree on specified terms'.[3] An offer may be express, which means either clearly written down or clearly stated, or it may be implied from conduct. Whatever its form, there must be an intention that the specified terms will become binding as soon as they are accepted by the offeree.

The law also distinguishes between an 'offer' and an 'invitation to treat'. The fundamental difference between the two is that an invitation to treat is merely an invitation to another party to make an offer.[4]

1.1 Auctions

By law, an auction constitutes an invitation to treat. An auction will typically involve an auctioneer calling for bids. In other words, the auctioneer is inviting participants to make an offer for the item that is being auctioned. The auctioneer is free to accept or reject the said offers. The bidder may also withdraw such offer before it is accepted.

This was illustrated in the case of *Payne v Cave*.[5] In this case, the defendant made the highest bid for the plaintiff's goods at an auction. Before the auctioneer's hammer fell, the defendant withdrew his bid. The

[1] See Robert Duxbury *Contract Law* 7 ed (2008) 7–11 for a discussion on the objective test for agreement.

[2] See *Lewis v Zimco* (1992) SJ (SC).

[3] Mphanza P Mvunga, Mumba Malila & Sangwani P Ng'ambi *Mvunga, Malila and Ng'ambi on Contracts* (2010) 1.

[4] See Edwin Peel *Treitel on the Law of Contract* 12 ed (2007) 12.

[5] (1789) 3 Term Rep 148.

court held that the bid was an offer, and the fall of the hammer would signify acceptance. The defendant was thus entitled to withdraw his offer at any time before the auctioneer's hammer fell, which he did. Therefore, the defendant was not bound to purchase the goods.

1.2 Display of goods

The display of goods is also regarded as an invitation to treat. Therefore it is the customer who makes an offer, which the shopkeeper is free to accept or reject. This was propounded in the case of *Fisher v Bell*,[6] which involved the display of a flick knife with a price tag in a shop window. It was illegal to offer these for sale under section 1(1) of the Restriction of Offensive Weapons Act 1959. The issue here was therefore whether the shopkeeper had in fact offered the knife for sale. The court held that the display of the knife in the shop window did not amount to an offer.

Similarly, in *Pharmaceutical Society of Great Britain v Boots Chemists*,[7] section 18(1) of the Pharmacy and Poisons Act 1933 stated that certain drugs could only be sold under the supervision of a registered pharmacist. The defendants operated a self-service system. This enabled customers to select the drugs they wanted, put them in a basket, and take them to the cashiers to pay.

The transaction at the cash desk was supervised by a pharmacist. The pharmacist had the power to prevent the removal of any drugs from the premises. The Pharmaceutical Society brought an action against the chemist. They contended that the self-service system was incongruous with the 1933 Act because the mere display of goods amounted to an offer, which the customer accepted when they placed the items in their basket. The unsupervised sale was thus completed at that point.

The Court of Appeal disagreed with this contention. It took the view that this was just a more organised way of doing what is already done in many shops. The court gave an example of a book seller who enables customers to have free access to what is in the shop. Once they have looked at different items, the customer chooses which one they wish to buy and takes it up to the assistant, thereby making an offer. (The assistant will invariably accept that offer.) It is then, and only then, that the transaction is completed.

---

[6] [1961] 1 QB 394.
[7] [1953] 1 All ER 482.

1.3 Advertisements

The general rule is that advertisement amounts to an invitation to treat rather than an offer. In the case of *Partridge v Crittenden*,[8] for example, it was an offence to offer for sale certain wild birds. The defendant ran an advertisement in a periodical which stated: 'Quality Bramblefinch cocks, Bramblefinch hens, 25s each.' The High Court held that this was not an offer but an invitation to treat.

However, from the case of *Carlill v Carbolic Smoke Ball Co*,[9] it can be seen that there are instances where an advertisement may amount to an offer. The defendants in this case had placed an advertisement for 'smoke balls' which prevented influenza. The advertisement stated: '£100 reward will be paid by the Carbolic Smoke Ball Company to any person who contracts the influenza after having used the ball three times daily for two weeks according to the printed directions supplied with each ball.'

In effect, the advertisement was offering to pay £100 to anyone who contracted influenza after using the ball. To show their sincerity in the matter, the company even deposited £1 000 with the Alliance Bank.

Despite using one of the balls, the plaintiff contracted influenza. The court held that the plaintiff was entitled to recover the £100. In the court's view, the offers made in the advertisement led to a unilateral contract which was accepted when the plaintiff fulfilled the conditions stipulated in the advertisement.

Similarly, in the case of *Lefkowitz v Great Minneapolis Surplus Stores*,[10] the defendants had issued an advertisement which stated: 'Saturday 9am sharp; 3 Brand new fur coats, worth $100, First come first served, $1 each.' Despite the fact that the plaintiff was one of the first three customers, the defendants refused to sell him a coat. This was on the basis that, under the house rules, the offer was only open to women. The court held that the advertisement constituted an offer and that the plaintiff had duly accepted it.

1.4 Statements of price

During transactions, a party may state the minimum price at which they are willing to sell a product. This does not, however, amount to an offer. In *Harvey v Facey*,[11] the plaintiffs had sent a telegraph querying the lowest cash price for 'Bumper Hall Pen'. The defendants responded, stating that

[8] [1968] 2 All ER 421.
[9] [1893] 1 QB 256.
[10] (1957) 86 NW 2d 689.
[11] [1893] AC 552.

their lowest price was '£900'. The plaintiffs responded with another telegraph, stating: 'We agree to buy . . . for £900 asked by you.' The Privy Council held that the defendants' initial response was not an offer. Given this fact, the plaintiffs' second telegraph could not have amounted to an acceptance.

In the more recent case of *Gibson v Manchester City Council*,[12] the council, which was dominated by the Conservative Party, had adopted a policy of selling council houses to tenants. To this effect, the council had written to the plaintiff, stating: 'The Corporation may be prepared to sell the house to you at the purchase price of [£2.180] . . . if you would like to make a formal application to buy your council house, please complete the enclosed application form and return it to me as soon as possible.'

This was filled in and sent back, along with an accompanying letter seeking a lower purchase price, on 5 March. This request was rejected by the council. On 18 March, the plaintiff wrote the council asking them to 'carry on with the purchase' as per his application. However, before contracts could be exchanged, the Labour Party took over the council and directed that no more council houses were to be sold unless they were legally bound to do so. The council thus declined to sell a house to the plaintiff.

The plaintiff initiated action against the council, seeking specific performance of the transaction. In his view, the letter from the council constituted an offer, which he had accepted through correspondence. The House of Lords rejected this argument. This was on the basis that the council had used the words 'may be prepared to sell' and invited the plaintiff to make a formal application to buy. In their view, this was not language consistent with an offer; rather, it was an invitation to treat.

2 ACCEPTANCE

An acceptance is 'an unqualified and unconditional assent, communicated by the offeree to the offeror, to all the terms of the offer, made with the intention of accepting'.[13] This may be communicated through words spoken or can be connoted from correspondence between the parties.

Acceptance may also be inferred through the conduct of the parties. In *Percy Trentham Ltd v Archital Luxfer Ltd*,[14] for example, the plaintiff built industrial units and subcontracted the windows to the defendant. Although

[12] [1979] 1 WLR 294.
[13] Duxbury n 1, 21.
[14] [1993] 1 Lloyd's Rep 25.

the work was completed and accordingly paid for, the windows had some defect. The plaintiff thus claimed damages from the defendant. The defendant argued that there was no matching offer and acceptance, despite the exchange of letters, phone calls and meetings between the parties. The court disagreed with this contention. In their opinion, this was of no consequence, as a contract could also be concluded through conduct.

Similarly, in the case of *Brogden v Metropolitan Railway Co*,[15] the Metropolitan Railway Company had sent an agreement to Brogden, who amended, signed and returned it. The court contended that the document which Brogden amended and returned amounted to a counter-offer. This counter-offer could be regarded as accepted either when the Metropolitan Railway Company ordered coal or when Brogden actually applied. It can thus be seen that the conduct of parties signifies approval of the agreement.

2.1 Counter-offers

A counter-offer occurs when the offeree, while purporting to accept the offer, introduces new terms which were not mentioned in the original offer. For example, if X offers to sell his Toyota Corolla for K50 000 and Y decides that she will accept the car at K45 000, this would amount to a counter-offer. X is free to either accept or reject that counter-offer. However, what needs to be underscored here is that Y's offer of K45 000 for the said car does not amount to an acceptance.

In essence, this was the case in *Hyde v Wrench*.[16] Wrench offered to sell his estate to Hyde for £1 000 on 6 June. On 27 June, Hyde offered Wrench £950, which was rejected by the latter. On 29 June, Hyde then offered Wrench £1 000. Wrench refused to sell, and Hyde sued him for breach of contract. The court held that there was no valid contract. Lord Langdale opined:

> I think there exists no valid binding contract between the parties for the purchase of the property. The Defendant offered to sell it for £1 000, and if that had been at once unconditionally accepted, there would undoubtedly have been a perfect binding contract; instead of that, the Plaintiff made an offer of his own, to purchase the property for £950, and he thereby rejected the offer previously made by the Defendant. I think that it was not afterwards competent for him to revive the proposal of the Defendant, by tendering an acceptance of it; and that, therefore, there exists no obligation of any sort between the parties; the demurrer must be allowed.

[15] (1877) 2 App Cas 666.
[16] (1840) 3 Beav 334.

The Supreme Court of Zambia took a similar line in the case of *Galaunia Farms Ltd v National Milling Company Ltd.*[17] The plaintiff had circulated a tender document. The defendant responded to this with an offer to purchase that year's wheat from the plaintiff. The tender document had been extensively amended by the defendant and upon its return was counter-signed by the plaintiff. In view of the amendments, the plaintiff proceeded to produce a 'cleaned-up contract', which was forwarded to the defendant for signing. The defendant, however, did not sign it. The issue arising was whether this cleaned-up contract amounted to an acceptance or a counter-offer.

The Supreme Court held that this amounted to a counter-offer. In his judgment, Silomba J opined that it could be successfully argued that the acceptance here was at variance with the terms of the offer. As such, the plaintiff did not accept all the terms contained in the offer. For this reason, the cleaned-up contract did not constitute acceptance of the offer. Therefore, there was no contract at all.

However, the law does make a distinction between a counter-offer on the one hand and a mere request for information on the other. In the case of *Stevenson v McLean,*[18] for instance, the defendant offered to sell iron to the plaintiff for the price of 40s per ton on a Saturday—an offer that was to remain open until Monday. On Monday at 10:00, the plaintiff responded by telegram, asking the defendant for credit terms. Later that day, at 13:34, the plaintiff sent another telegram, this time accepting the defendant's offer. However, the defendant had sent a telegram to the plaintiff at 13:25, stating that they had sold the iron to a third party. This was only received at 13:46.

The plaintiff sued for breach of contract. The defendant argued that the plaintiff's telegram was a counter-offer and, as such, did not constitute an acceptance. The court rejected this argument on the basis that the plaintiff's first telegram was a mere enquiry as opposed to a counter-offer. A binding contract was thus made when the plaintiff sent its second telegram.

2.2 Battle of the forms

Most businesses entering into transactions will typically have their own standard terms. An example may be when you are seeking to purchase furniture from a shop. Their standard terms may be printed on the relevant company documentation such as an invoice or receipt. The purpose of this is to avoid entering into specific negotiations every time they enter into a contract.

---

[17] [2002] ZMHC 2.

[18] (1880) 5 QBD 346.

The battle of the forms may arise where the furniture shop in our example offers its own standard terms but the customer purports to accept it with their own standard terms. If the two sets of terms are incongruous with one another, the question arises as to whether there is a contract at all. At first glance it would appear not because, technically, the acceptance amounts to a counter-offer. However, if the furniture shop appears to accept the customer's standard terms by conduct, there will be a contract.

The case of *Butler Machine Tool v Excell-o-Corp*[19] is instructive in this regard. The plaintiffs offered to sell a machine to the defendants. However, when the defendants accepted, they did so on terms and conditions that were at variance with those of the plaintiffs. At the foot of their order was a tear-off slip which stated: 'We accept your order on the Terms and Conditions stated thereon.' The plaintiffs signed and returned that slip, writing 'your official order . . . is being entered in accordance with our revised quotation . . .'. The question before the Court of Appeal was which set of terms the contract was made on. Lord Denning contended:

> [I]n most cases when there is a 'battle of forms', there is a contract as soon as the last of the forms is sent and received without objection being taken to it . . . In some cases the battle is won by the man who fires the last shot. He is the man who puts forward the latest terms and conditions: and, if they are not objected to by the other party, he may be taken to have agreed to them . . . In some cases the battle is won by the man who gets the blow in first. If he offers to sell at a named price on the terms and conditions stated on the back: and the buyer orders the goods purporting to accept the offer—on an order form with his own different terms and conditions on the back—then if the difference is so material that it would affect the price, the buyer ought not to be allowed to take advantage of the difference unless he draws it specifically to the attention of the seller. There are yet other cases where the battle depends on the shots fired on both sides. There is a concluded contract but the forms vary. The terms and conditions of both parties are to be construed together. If they can be reconciled so as to give a harmonious result, all well and good. If differences are irreconcilable—so that they are mutually contradictory—then the conflicting terms may have to be scrapped and replaced by a reasonable implication.

Lord Denning took the view that the plaintiffs' acknowledgement through the tear-off slip was the determinant in this case. It was clear from this that the contract in this case was on the buyer's terms, not the seller's.

2.3 Tenders

When a person invites tenders, they are effectively binding themselves to accept either the highest bid or the lowest one. In *Harvela Investments v Royal Trust Co of Canada*,[20] the Royal Trust had invited offers by sealed

[19] [1979] 1 WLR 401.
[20] [1986] AC 207.

tender for sales in the company. They undertook that they would accept the highest offer. Harvela made a bid of $2 175 000. Sir Leonard Outerbridge placed a bid of $2 100 000 or $100 000 in excess of any other offer. Although the Royal Trust accepted Sir Leonard's offer, the trial judge found in favour of Harvela when this transaction was challenged.

The House of Lords held that the referential bid rendered by Sir Leonard was in fact invalid because it was inconsistent with the fixed bidding sale. The Royal Trust was thus obliged to sell its shares to Harvela because the invitation to tender amounted to a unilateral offer to accept the highest bid—which was accepted by Harvela, who submitted the highest bid.

Similarly, in *Blackpool Aero Club v Blackpool Borough Council*,[21] the defendant had invited tenders to operate an airport. These were to be submitted by noon on a given date. The plaintiff delivered their tender by hand at 11:00. However, it was erroneously recorded as having been received late. As a result, it was not considered.

The plaintiff sued on the basis that there was a guarantee that all tenders submitted before the fixed date would be considered. The judge awarded damages for negligence and damages for breach of contract at first instance. The council's subsequent appeal was dismissed by the Court of Appeal. Bingham LJ opined: '[T]enders are solicited from selected parties all of them known to the invitor, and where a local authority's invitation prescribes a clear, orderly and familiar procedure . . . the invitee is in my judgement protected at least to this extent.' If an invitee submits a tender that conforms to the terms stipulated before the deadline, they are entitled as a matter of contractual right to have their tender considered with all the other tenders.

2.4 Communication with the offeror

The offeree must communicate their acceptance to the offeror—one cannot accept in the abstract. Communication occurs once the acceptance is brought to the attention of the offeror. This was explained by Denning LJ in *Entores v Miles Far East Corp*.[22] He opined:

> Suppose, for instance, that I shout an offer to a man across a river or a courtyard but I do not hear his reply because it is drowned by an aircraft flying overhead. There is no contract at that moment. If he wishes to make a contract, he must wait till the aircraft is gone and then shout back his acceptance so that I can hear what he says. Not until I have his answer am I bound.

---

[21] [1990] 3 All ER 25.
[22] [1955] 2 All ER 493.

This case involved the making of a contract over the telephone. Denning LJ explained that if an offer is made over the telephone and the line goes dead at the crucial moment when acceptance is rendered, then such acceptance has not been communicated. Thus, if the offeree wishes to make a contract, they must dial that line again and make sure that the offeror hears the acceptance.

2.5 Who can accept?

The acceptance may only be communicated by the offeree or someone authorised by the offeree. Thus, there can be no valid acceptance in the event that someone accepts on behalf of the offeree without their authorisation. This was affirmed in the case of *Powell v Lee*,[23] which concerned the plaintiff applying for a job as headmaster. The managers had initially decided to appoint the plaintiff. In fact, one of them even communicated acceptance to him without authorisation. The managers, however, decided later to appoint someone else for the job.

When the plaintiff sued, the court held that this did not constitute a binding contract. This was because the manager who had communicated the acceptance was not authorised to do so.

2.6 Silence

The common law also espouses that silence cannot amount to acceptance. This was illustrated in *Felthouse v Bindley*.[24] The plaintiff in this case had discussed the possibility of purchasing a horse from his nephew. The plaintiff thus wrote to his nephew, stating: 'If I hear no more about him, I consider the horse mine . . .'

Although his nephew did not reply to this letter, he did intend to sell the horse to the plaintiff. When the defendant auctioneer was having a sale, the nephew expressly told him not to sell it. By mistake, however, the defendant did sell the horse. The plaintiff's action in the tort of conversion could only succeed if he could show that the horse was his. The court held that his nephew's silence could not amount to acceptance. For this reason, the horse was not his.

A similar position on silence was taken by the Supreme Court of Zambia in the case of *Galaunia Farms v National Milling*. They opined that silence does not amount to an acceptance of a counter-offer. They did, however, go

[23] (1908) 99 LT 284.
[24] (1862) 11 CB (NS) 869.

on to say that there may be other facts which, if taken conjunctively with the offeree's silence, may constitute acceptance.

2.7 Instantaneous modes of communication

Where methods of communication are instantaneous, the contract is deemed to be complete when acceptance is received by the offeror. This was established in the case of *Entores v Miles Far East Corporation.*[25] This case involved the plaintiffs in London, who had made an offer by Telex to the defendants in Holland. The defendants then communicated their acceptance to the plaintiffs' Telex machine in London. When a dispute arose, the Court of Appeal had to decide where the contract had been completed. The Court of Appeal held that the contract was complete when acceptance was received by the offeror.

Similarly, in *Tenax Steamship Company Limited v Owners of The Brimnes,*[26] the defendants had hired a ship from the plaintiff. The plaintiff complained of a breach of the contract via Telex to the defendants and indicated that they would be withdrawing the ship from service. This message was sent between 17:30 and 18:00. However, the defendants did not see the message until the next morning. The court held that the Telex must be regarded as having been received at 17:45. As far as the court was concerned, the Telex had been sent during business hours.

In *Brinkibon v Stahag Stahl,*[27] an English company had sent a Telex to Vienna in which they accepted the terms of the sale offered by the sellers. The buyers later issued a writ claiming damages for breach of contract. The House of Lords held that the writ should be set aside. Lord Wilberforce opined:

> Since 1955 the use of Telex communication has been greatly expanded, and there are many variants on it. The senders and recipients may not be the principals to the contemplated contract. They may be servants or agents with limited authority. The message may not reach, or be intended to reach, the designated recipient immediately: messages may be sent out of office hours, or at night, with the intention, or on the assumption that they will be read at a later time. There may be some error or default at the recipient's end which prevents receipt at the time contemplated and believed in by the sender. The message may have been sent and/or received through machines operated by third persons. And many other variants may occur. No universal rule can cover all such cases; they must be resolved by reference to the intentions of the parties, by sound business practice and in some cases by a judgement where the risks should lie.

[25] [1955] 2 QB 327.
[26] [1975] QB 929.
[27] [1983] 2 AC 34.

Thus, each case must be decided on its own facts. In practice, however, the decision in *Brinkibon* suggests that acceptance will take effect at the time when the offeree would reasonably expect the acceptance to have been read.

2.8 The postal rule

Acceptance rendered through mail is deemed to have been communicated once the letter has been posted.[28] In *Household Fire Insurance Co v Grant*,[29] the defendant applied for shares in the plaintiff company. Although a letter of allotment of shares was posted, the defendant never received it. When the company went into liquidation, Grant was asked as a shareholder to contribute the amount still outstanding on the shares he had. The issue here was whether Grant could be bound if he never received the letter. The Court of Appeal held that he was. It would thus appear that the postal rule applies even though the defendant has not received the letter of acceptance.[30]

The postal rule also applies to communications of acceptance by cable, for example telegram. As seen in the case of *Entores*, however, this rule will not apply to instantaneous modes of communication such as telephone, Telex, email and fax. In addition to this, the postal rule will not apply in instances where the letter has not been posted properly,[31] nor will it apply if the letter has been misaddressed.[32] Moreover, the postal rule does not apply in situations where terms of the offer expressly exclude it.[33] It will also not apply where the rule would produce a 'manifest inconvenience or absurdity'.[34]

2.9 Method of acceptance

It would appear that if one particular method of acceptance is prescribed by either party, without an express declaration as to whether other methods are excluded, those other methods will suffice. This is provided that they are

[28] See generally *Adams v Lindsell* (1818) 1 B & Ald 681.

[29] (1879) 4 Ex D 216.

[30] See however the dissenting judgment of Bramwell LJ, who spoke of the difficulties with the postal rule.

[31] See *Re London and Northern Bank* [1900] 1 Ch 220.

[32] Although there is no authority on this, see the analogous case of *Getreide-Import-Gesellschaft MBH v Continmar SA Compania Industrial Commercial y Maritima* [1953] 2 All ER 223.

[33] See *Holwell Securities v Hughes* [1974] 1 WLR 155.

[34] Ibid.

equally advantageous. In *Tinn v Hoffman*,[35] the method of acceptance was by return of post. Honeyman J opined:

> That does not mean exclusively a reply by letter or return of post, but you may reply by telegram or by verbal message or by any other means not later than a letter written by return of post.

In *Yates Building Co v Pulleyn Ltd*,[36] the defendant granted the plaintiff an option to buy land. This option was to be exercised in writing and sent via 'registered or recorded delivery post'. The plaintiff opted to send the acceptance letter by ordinary post, which the defendant refused to accept as valid. The court rejected this position and held that the method of acceptance was valid and did not disadvantage the offeror in any way. The method stipulated was simply a means of ensuring that the letter was delivered.

2.10 Knowledge of the offer

In order to accept an offer, the offeree must have knowledge of such offer. However, even with knowledge of this offer, the offeree may sometimes accept the offer with motives that are wholly extrinsic to the offer. In such a situation, the acceptance has no effect. An illustrative case is *R v Clarke*.[37] Clarke gave information leading to the capture and conviction of certain murderers after the government had offered a reward in respect of the same. By his own admission, he only offered this information only to clear his own name in a murder case. However, he then proceeded to sue the government for the reward. The High Court dismissed the case. Higgins J opined:

> Clarke had seen the offer, indeed; but it was not present to his mind—he had forgotten it, and gave no consideration to it, in his intense excitement as to his own danger. There cannot be assent without knowledge of the offer; and ignorance of the offer is the same thing whether it is due to never hearing of it or forgetting it after hearing.

This can be contrasted with *Williams v Carwardine*.[38] The defendant here also offered a reward leading to the conviction of a murderer. The plaintiff was aware of the offer; however, she provided information that the murderer was her husband after he had beaten her because she thought she did not have long to live and wished to clear her conscience.

Parke J opined: '[T]he motive was the state of her own feelings. My opinion is, the motive is not material.' This view was reaffirmed by the

[35] (1873) 29 LT 271.
[36] (1975) 119 SJ 370.
[37] (1927) 40 CLR 227.
[38] (1833) 5 Car & P 566.

Court of the King's Bench.[39] Thus, where the offeree's acceptance is only partly influenced by some extraneous factor, it may still be effective.

3 TERMINATION OF THE OFFER

3.1 Acceptance and rejection

Once the offeree has accepted an offer, a binding contract is formed between the parties. The offer thus ends. Indeed, the offer may also be terminated if the offeree rejects it. For example, if one party says, 'I am selling my Chilenje house for K250 000', and the other party says, 'No thank you', the offer is effectively terminated. The other party cannot retract this rejection. They will simply have to wait for another offer.

3.2 Revocation

As a general rule, revocation of an offer is not effective until it has been received. In *Byrne v Van Tienhoven*,[40] the defendant posted a letter offering goods for sale on 1 October. The defendant revoked the offer on 8 October. However, this did not arrive until 20 October. The plaintiff accepted the offer by telegram on 11 October. Further, on 15 October, the plaintiff also sent a letter confirming acceptance. The court held that the revocation was not effective until 20 October, when it was received by the plaintiff.

It would appear, however, that offers made in error may be withdrawn at any time. This was certainly established in *Lusaka City Council, National Airports Corporation v Mwamba and 4 Others*.[41]

Further, the revocation does not necessarily have to be communicated personally to the offeree. Conveying the information through a reliable third party will suffice.[42] Moreover, if one wishes to revoke an offer, this must be communicated through the same channels that the offeror used when making the offer. This was established in the case of *Shuey v United States*.[43]

Once the offeree has commenced a task within a reasonable time, the offeror cannot revoke their offer. This was established in the case of *Errington v Errington*.[44] A father purchased a house on mortgage for his

[39] Littledale J said 'If the person knows of the handbill and does the thing, that is quite enough', whereas Patteson J said 'We cannot go into the plaintiff's motives'.
[40] (1880) 5 CPD 344.
[41] SCZ Judgment 21 of 1999.
[42] *Dickinson v Dodds* (1876) 2 Ch D 463.
[43] [1875] 92 US 73.
[44] [1952] 1 KB 290.

son and daughter-in-law. He promised them that they could have the house once they had paid off the mortgage. Although they had begun to pay off their mortgage, the father died before they could finish. His widow claimed the house. The daughter-in-law was granted possession of the house at first instance. This was upheld by the Court of Appeal. Denning LJ opined:

> The father's promise was a unilateral contract—a promise of the house in return for their act of paying the instalments. It could not be revoked by him once the couple entered on performance of the act, but it would cease to bind him if they left it incomplete and unperformed, which they have not done. If that was the position during the father's lifetime, so it must be after his death. If the daughter-in-law continues to pay all the building society instalments, the couple will be entitled to have the property transferred to them as soon as the mortgage is paid off; but if she does not do so, then the building society will claim the instalments from the father's estate and the estate will have to pay them. I cannot think that in those circumstances the estate would be bound to transfer the house to them, any more than the father himself would have been.

In *Daulia v Four Millbank Nominees*,[45] the court held that under unilateral contracts, the offeror is entitled to require full performance of the condition imposed. Goff LJ further stated:

> That must be subject to one important qualification—there must be an implied obligation on the part of the offeror not to prevent the condition being satisfied, an obligation which arises as soon as the offeree starts to perform. Until then the offeror can revoke the whole thing, but once the offeree has embarked on performance, it is too late for the offeror to revoke his offer.

3.3 Lapse of time

An offer may also be terminated by lapse of time: if the offer stipulates that it is open for a specific period, it is automatically terminated when that time limit elapses. If no time limit is set, the offer is typically open for a reasonable period of time.

In *Ramsgate Victoria Hotel v Montefiore*,[46] the defendant offered to purchase shares in the plaintiff company on 8 June. This offer was accepted by the plaintiff on 23 November. The defendant no longer wanted them and thus refused to pay. The court held that the six-month delay between the offer in June and the acceptance in November was unreasonable. Therefore, the offer had lapsed.

3.4 Failure of a condition

An offer may also be made subject to conditions, which may be expressly stated or implied by the circumstances. Failure to satisfy such a condition

[45] [1978] 2 All ER 557.
[46] (1866) LR 1 Ex 109.

means that the offer is incapable of being accepted. In *Financings Ltd v Stimson*,[47] the defendant signed a form at the premises of a dealer. Under this agreement, the defendant offered to take a car on hire-purchase terms from the plaintiff. He paid a deposit and was allowed to take the car away.

However, the defendant was not satisfied with it and decided to return it to the dealer. The car was then stolen from the dealer's premises and damaged. The plaintiff, who had not been told that the defendant had returned the car, signed the hire-purchase agreement.

The Court of Appeal held that the defendant's offer had been revoked when he returned the car to the dealer, because there was an express provision which stipulated that the defendant had to examine the car and be satisfied that it was in good order and condition. As this condition had not been fulfilled, the acceptance was not valid.

3.5 Death

The offer is also terminated once the offeree is made aware of the offeror's death. If the offeree is unaware of the offeror's death and there is no personal element involved, then the offer is still capable of being accepted. This was established in *Bradbury v Morgan*.[48]

---

[47] [1962] 3 All ER 386.
[48] (1862) 1 H & C 249.

Chapter 3

CONSIDERATION

Offer and acceptance alone are not sufficient to form a binding contract. There must also be consideration. Consideration is 'some right, interest, profit or benefit accruing to one party, or some forbearance, detriment, loss or responsibility given, suffered or undertaken by the other'.[1] Further, in *Dunlop v Selfridge Ltd*,[2] consideration was defined as follows: 'An act or forbearance of one party, or the promise thereof, is the price for which the promise of the other is bought, and the promise thus given for value is enforceable.' The aim of this chapter is to discuss the rules governing consideration.

1 RULES GOVERNING CONSIDERATION

1.1 Consideration must not be past

If one party has performed an act voluntarily and the other party subsequently makes a promise, the consideration is said to be past. When this occurs, it means that there is no consideration; consequently, there can be no valid contract between the parties. Thus, in *Re McArdle*,[3] a promise to pay £488 for decorative work done on a house was not enforceable. This was because all the work had been done before the promise was made and therefore amounted to past consideration.

1.2 Exceptions to this rule

1.2.1 *Previous request*

There are, however, exceptions to this general rule. The first exception is where a previous request has been made. This can occur where the promissor asks the other party to provide goods or services and then subsequently makes a promise. An illustrating case is *Lampleigh v Braithwaite*.[4] Braithwaite had committed murder and asked Lampleigh to obtain a pardon for him.

---

[1] Per Lush J in *Curie v Misa* (1875) LR 10 Exch 153.

[2] [1915] AC 847.

[3] [1951] 1 All ER 905.

[4] (1615) Hob 105.

Once Lampleigh had obtained this pardon, Braithwaite then promised to pay him £100 for his trouble. The court held that although Lampleigh's consideration was past, Braithwaite's pay could be linked to his earlier request and be treated as one agreement. Therefore, it can be implied that at the time of Braithwaite's request, Lampleigh would be paid.

1.2.2 *Business situations*

Another exception to this rule is when something is done in a business context and there is a clear understanding by both parties that the goods or services provided will be paid for. In such an instance past consideration will be valid.

In *Re Casey's Patents*,[5] A and B owned a patent, and C was the manager who had worked on it for two years. Because of his help in developing the patent, A and B promised C that he would have a one-third share in the invention. The patents were transferred to C. Later, however, A and B claimed their return.

The court held that C could rely on the agreement. This was because the transaction had been undertaken in a business context at the request of A and B. Further, it had been understood by both sides that C would be paid; the subsequent promise to pay merely fixed the amount.[6]

1.3 Consideration must be sufficient but need not be adequate

The courts do not concern themselves with whether consideration is adequate in the circumstances. All they are concerned with is whether consideration has been given in exchange for a promise.

In *Chappell & Co Ltd v Nestle Co Ltd*,[7] Nestle ran a special offer under which the public could obtain a music record by sending in three wrappers from Nestle's chocolate bars. In addition to this, they would need to pay some money. Chappell, the copyright owner, sued, claiming that there had been an infringement of their copyright. The issue that arose was whether the three wrappers were part of consideration. The court held that they did amount to consideration despite the fact that they were thrown away once

[5] [1892] 1 Ch 104.

[6] See also *Pao On v Lau Yiu Long* [1980] AC 614, where Lord Scarman opined that: 'An act done before the giving of a promise to make a payment or to confer some other benefit can sometimes be consideration for the promise. The act must have been done at the promisors' request: the parties must have understood that the act was to be remunerated either by a payment or the conferment of some other benefit: and payment, or the conferment of a benefit, must have been legally enforceable had it been promised in advance.'

[7] [1960] AC 87.

received. As far as the court was concerned: 'A contracting party can stipulate for whatever consideration he chooses.'[8]

1.4 Consideration must move from the promisee

In order to enforce the contract, the promisee must prove that the consideration moved from them, ie that the consideration was provided by them: showing that someone else has provided the consideration will not suffice. This was certainly the case in *Price v Easton*,[9] where the defendant made a contract with Party X in return for receiving services from the latter. The defendant was to pay a sum of £19. Despite Party X completing the work, the defendant did not pay. The plaintiff thus sued the defendant. The court held that Price's claim must fail because he had not provided consideration.

1.5 Forbearance to sue

When one promises to forgo their right to sue in civil proceedings, this too can constitute good consideration. In *Alliance Bank v Broom*,[10] the defendant owed an unsecured debt to the plaintiff. When the plaintiff asked for security, the defendant promised that he would provide some goods as surety. In return, the plaintiff promised not to sue the defendant.

When the defendant failed to provide the goods, the plaintiff tried to enforce the agreement for the security. The issue was whether the plaintiff had provided consideration in its actual forbearance from suing. The court held that by not suing, the plaintiff had shown forbearance, which, in the court's view, constituted consideration. As such, the agreement to provide security was binding.

1.6 Existing public duty

As a general rule, performance of an existing public duty does not constitute sufficient consideration. The traditional authority to support this proposition is *Collins v Godefroy*.[11] The defendant promised to pay the plaintiff if he would attend court and give evidence on the former's behalf. The plaintiff was subpoenaed by the court, but nonetheless sued for payment. The court held that since the plaintiff was under a legal duty to attend court, he had not provided consideration.

---

[8] Per Lord Somervell.
[9] (1833) 4 B & Ad 433.
[10] (1864) 2 Dr & Sm 289.
[11] (1831) 1 B & Ad 950.

The exception to this rule is where the promisee exceeds their public duty. In *Glassbrook Brothers v Glamorgan County Council*,[12] the court held that extra protection provided by the police to a coal mine did amount to good consideration.

1.7 Existing contractual duty

The old position was that performance of a contractual obligation that was already in existence did not amount to good consideration. This classic position was espoused in the case of *Stilk v Myrick*.[13] In this case, two out of 11 sailors deserted a ship. The ship captain thus promised to pay the remaining crew extra money if they sailed the ship back. Later, however, the captain refused to pay. The court held that since the sailors were already bound by their contract to sail back, their later promise to continue with the voyage did not amount to valid consideration. As such, the captain was not obliged to pay the extra money he had promised.

However, this decision can be contrasted with that in *Hartley v Ponsonby*,[14] where 19 out of 36 crew had deserted a ship. The captain of this ship promised to pay the remaining crew extra money if they sailed the ship back. However, just as in the previous case, the captain refused to disburse this extra money once they did sail back. The captain contended that the sailors were simply doing their jobs. The court held in this instance that the sailors were entitled to the money. This was owing to the fact that the ship was so seriously undermanned that the rest of the journey had become extremely hazardous. The conditions had thus become so dangerous that the sailors were going beyond the scope of their normal duties.

The rule in *Stilk v Myrick* has since been altered by the case of *Williams v Roffey Bros Ltd*.[15] Roffey had been contracted to refurbish a block of flats. He subcontracted the carpentry work to Williams. However, once the work commenced, it became apparent to Williams that they had underestimated the cost of the work.

Consequently, Roffey agreed to pay Williams an extra amount per flat. When Williams completed the work on more flats, he did not receive full payment and thus brought an action for damages. In the Court of Appeal, Roffey argued that Williams was doing what he was contractually bound to do in the first place, and therefore he had not provided consideration. The

---

12 [1925] AC 270.
13 (1809) 2 Camp 317.
14 (1857) 7 E & B 872.
15 [1991] 1 QB 1.

Court of Appeal disagreed and held that there had been good consideration. For this reason, Roffey's promise was binding. There were practical benefits to be derived by Roffey: for example, because Williams continued doing his work, Roffey avoided penalties for delay in completion, and Roffey did not have to go through the trouble of engaging another carpenter to finish the work.

1.8 Existing contractual duty owed to a third party

Existing contractual duty owed to a third party also amounts to good consideration. Thus, if A makes a promise to B to perform a duty he already owes to C, under an existing contract with C, then this still amounts to good consideration. In *Scotson v Pegg*,[16] Scotson was contracted to deliver coal to X or to X's order. X had sold the coal to Pegg and ordered Scotson to deliver it to him. Pegg then promised Scotson that he would unload it at a fixed rate. The court held that Scotson's delivery was a benefit to Pegg and therefore amounted to valid consideration.

2 PART-PAYMENT OF A DEBT

2.1 The general rule

The rule established in *Pinnel's Case*[17] is that part-payment of a debt is not good consideration for a promise to forgo the balance. Lord Coke stated: 'Payment of a lesser sum on the day [it is due to be paid] cannot be any satisfaction for the whole, because it appears to the judges that by no possibility a lesser sum can be satisfaction to the [claimant] for a greater sum.'

The rule in *Pinnel* was reaffirmed by the House of Lords in *Foakes v Beer*.[18] Dr Foakes owed Mrs Beer £2 090.19sh. Mrs Beer had obtained a judgment against Dr Foakes, who then asked for time to pay. Mrs Beer agreed not to take further action in the matter, provided that Dr Foakes pay £500 immediately and then the rest in half-yearly instalments of £150. He duly kept his end of the bargain. However, Mrs Beer then realised that she had not charged the interest of 4% that, by statute, was always due on a judgment debt.

When Dr Foakes refused to pay this sum, Mrs Beer applied for leave to sue. She contended that Dr Foakes had given no consideration for the

[16] (1861) 6 H & N 295.
[17] (1602) 5 CoRep 117a.
[18] (1884) 9 App Cas 605.

agreement. The House of Lords held that she was entitled to the interest. The promise to pay a debt was not deemed to be sufficient consideration. This is because there was no additional benefit moving from Dr Foakes to Mrs Beer that was not already owed to her.[19]

2.2 Part-payment of the debt by a third party

If part-payment is offered by a third party and is accepted by the creditor, the law seems to suggest that this is good consideration. In *Hirachand Punamchand v Temple*,[20] a father had paid a smaller sum to a money lender in order to cover his son's debts. Although the lender did initially accept this amount in full settlement, he later sued for the balance. The court held that this part-payment amounted to valid consideration.

2.3 Composition agreements

Composition agreements occur when a debtor and a group of creditors agree to accept a percentage of the former's debt in full settlement. In such instances, the rule in *Pinnel's Case* will not apply.[21]

3 PROMISSORY ESTOPPEL

3.1 Introduction

Promissory estoppel is another exception to the rule in *Pinnel's Case*. Under this principle, if the promissor makes an undertaking which is acted on by another person, the promissor is prevented (or estopped) from going back on that promise. This is so even where the other person has not provided consideration.

In *Central London Property Trust Ltd v High Trees House Ltd*,[22] the plaintiffs had granted a 99-year lease on a block of flats at an annual rent of £2 500 to the defendants in 1937. When World War II broke out in 1939, it meant that the defendants could not obtain enough tenants. The plaintiffs thus reduced their rent to £1 250 in 1940. Once the war had ended in 1945, all the flats were occupied. The plaintiffs thus sued to recover arrears of rent as fixed by the 1937 agreement for the last two quarters of 1945.

Denning J held that there was a promise which the promissor knew would be acted on by the person to whom it was made. Such a promise is

[19] See also *Zambia State Insurance Corporation Ltd and Helmos Transport Ltd v Chanda (Trading as Link Express Motorways)* (1990–1992) ZR 175.
[20] [1911] 2 KB 330.
[21] *Wood v Robarts* (1818) 2 Stark 417.
[22] [1947] 1 KB 130.

enforceable despite lack of consideration. Such a situation gives rise to an estoppel. He further contended that, indeed, the plaintiffs in this case had made a binding promise. However, from the evidence, it would appear that this promise only applied during the war. Therefore, after the war had ended, the defendants were liable for the full rent.

3.2 Requirements

In order for promissory estoppel to apply, certain elements must be fulfilled. The first is that there must be an existing legal relationship. Secondly, there must be a clear and unambiguous promise. Thirdly, there must be reliance and, finally, it must be inequitable to revert.

3.2.1 *Contractual/legal relationship*

There must be some legal or contractual relationship between the plaintiff and the defendant. However, this is not always necessary, and this was highlighted by Donaldson J in *Durham Fancy Goods v Michael Jackson (Fancy Goods)*.[23] He stated that an existing contractual relationship is not essential, provided that there was 'a pre-existing legal relationship which could, in certain circumstances, give rise to liabilities and penalties'.

3.2.2 *Promise*

There must also be a clear and unambiguous promise made by the promissor. This would be a clear and unequivocal statement on the part of the promissor that they would not enforce their legal rights.[24] This can also be implied by conduct, as was illustrated in *Hughes v Metropolitan Railway Co*.[25]

3.2.3 *Reliance*

The promisee must also have acted in reliance on the promise. Although the classic position is that the promisee should be placed in a worse position than they would have been had the promise never been made, this position seems to have been altered by the case of *Alan Co Ltd v El Nasr Export & Import Co*.[26] In this case, Lord Denning asserted that detriment was not a necessary element of promissory estoppel. He was of the view that the promisee 'must have been led to act differently from what he otherwise would have done'.

[23] [1968] 2 QB 839.
[24] *The Scaptrade* [1983] QB 529.
[25] (1877) 2 App Cas 439.
[26] [1972] 2 QB 189.

3.2.4 *Inequitable to revert*

It must also be inequitable for the promissor to go back on their promise. Whether a matter is inequitable is decided on a case-by-case basis.

In *D & C Builders v Rees*,[27] the plaintiff building company had completed some work for Mr Rees. The latter thus owed the company £482. The company, which had been undergoing severe financial difficulties for months, pressed Mr Rees for payment.

These problems came to the attention of Mrs Rees, who contacted the company and offered £300 in full settlement. Further, she stated that if the company refused this offer, they would receive nothing. Although the company reluctantly accepted a cheque for £300, they later sued for the balance. The Court of Appeal held that the company was entitled to recover the balance. This was based more on the rule in *Pinnel*'s *Case* and *Foakes v Beer*.

Lord Denning, however, went on to discuss whether the defendant could have raised the defence of promissory estoppel. He contended that the principle could be applied 'not only so as to suspend strict legal rights, but also so as to preclude the enforcement of them'. He went on to say that the creditor is precluded from enforcing their strict legal rights in instances where it would be inequitable to do so.

He considered Mrs Rees' conduct and found that she had acted inequitably in that she had put undue pressure on the creditor. She was making a threat to break the contract and did so to compel the creditor to do what she was unwilling to do. In summary, he said 'no person can insist on a settlement procured by intimidation'.

3.3 A shield or a sword?

Traditionally, promissory estoppel could only be raised as a defence. In other words, it was deemed to be 'as a shield and not a sword'.[28] It therefore follows that it cannot found a cause of action.[29] Further, there are questions as to whether the doctrine extinguishes rights or merely suspends them. Most authorities seem to suggest that the doctrine merely suspends them.[30]

---

[27] [1965] 2 QB 617.

[28] See *Coombe v Coombe* [1951] 2 KB 215.

[29] See, however, *Waltons Stores v Maher* (1988) 76 ALR 513, which illustrates the different view taken by the Australian courts.

[30] See generally *Tool Metal Manufacture Co Ltd v Tungsten Electric Co Ltd* [1955] 2 All ER 657.

Chapter 4

INTENTION TO CREATE LEGAL RELATIONS

The final element in formation of contract is that the parties must intend for their agreement to be legally binding. Generally, this is determined by applying an objective test and judging the parties by what was said and done. There are two main headings under 'intention to create legal relations'. The first deals with social and domestic agreements. Under these, the general presumption is that there is no intention to create legal relations. The second heading deals with business agreements. The general presumption is that there is an intention to be bound under these agreements.

1 SOCIAL AND DOMESTIC AGREEMENTS

1.1 Husband and wife living together

A contract between a husband and wife living together generally does not give rise to an intention to create legal relations. This was illustrated in *Balfour v Balfour*.[1] The defendant worked in Ceylon and went on holiday to England with his wife. He returned to Ceylon alone because his wife remained in England for health reasons. The defendant promised to pay the plaintiff £30 per month as maintenance. He failed to keep up payments when the marriage ended, and so the plaintiff sued. The court held that this action could not succeed. This was because there was no intention to create legal relations. There was a general presumption that such domestic agreements are not intended to create legal relations, and the plaintiff had failed to rebut that presumption.

1.2 Where spouses are not living together in amity

One exception to this rule is where the spouses are not living together in amity. In *Merritt v Merritt*,[2] a husband left his wife and the two parties met to make arrangements for the future. The husband agreed to pay his wife a sum of £40 per month as maintenance. Out of this amount the wife was to

[1] [1919] 2 KB 571.
[2] [1970] 1 WLR 1211.

pay the mortgage. It was agreed that once the mortgage was paid off, he would transfer the house from their joint names into her name. This was all written down on paper. When the time came to transfer the house, however, he refused to do so. The court held in this case that there was an enforceable agreement.

Lord Denning opined that the principle espoused in *Balfour v Balfour* did not apply here because the parties were not living in amity but were separated. In such a situation, it is presumed that they intended to create legal relations.

1.3 Where the social agreement has consequences

Social agreements with consequences are also enforceable. An illustrating case is *Parker v Clarke*.[3] The Parkers and the Clarkes had made an agreement under which the former would sell their home and move in with the latter. They would then share the bills, and the Clarkes would eventually leave their home to the Parkers. The Parkers accordingly sold their home and moved in with the Clarkes. Mr Clarke even proceeded to change his will so that his home would be left to the Parkers.

The couples later fell out and the Parkers were asked to leave. Subsequently, the Parkers claimed damages for breach of contract. The court held that the exchange of letters between the two signified that the two couples were serious about the agreement and, as such, intended it to be legally binding. This was underscored by the fact that the Parkers sold their home and that Mr Clarke changed his will. Thus, the Parkers were entitled to damages.[4]

1.4 Parents and children

The presumption is that agreements between children and their parents are not intended to create legal relations. In *Jones v Padavatton*,[5] a mother offered a monthly allowance to her daughter. This was on the condition that she would give up her job in America and come to England and study to become a barrister.

Due to accommodation problems, the mother purchased her daughter a home in London, where she lived and received rentals from other lodgers.

---

[3] [1960] 1 All ER 93.

[4] See also *Tanner v Tanner* [1975] 1 WLR 1346, where a man had promised his partner (whom he was not married to) that the house in which they had lived together should be available for her and the couple's children. The court held that this promise had contractual force because the woman moved out of her flat in reliance on this promise.

[5] [1969] 2 All ER 616.

In 1967, they had a disagreement and the mother claimed the home, even though her daughter had not yet passed half of her exams. The court held that the first agreement to study was a family agreement and therefore was not intended to create legal relations. Even if it was, it could only be deemed to run for a reasonable period of time, in this case five years.

However, case law suggests that where the parties to an agreement share a household but are not related, the courts will examine all the circumstances of the case. In *Simpkins v Pays*,[6] the defendant shared a house with her granddaughter and a paying lodger. They had all contributed a one-third stake in entering a fashion competition organised by the Sunday newspaper. They had entered the said competition in the defendant's name and had done this quite regularly. One week, they won a prize of £750. However, the defendant refused to share the prize. The plaintiff therefore sued. The court held that the presence of the plaintiff, who was essentially an outsider, rebutted the presumption that the agreement was not intended to create legal relations.

2 BUSINESS OR COMMERCIAL AGREEMENTS

The general presumption when it comes to business or commercial agreements is that the parties intend to create legal relations. This, of course, is a rebuttable presumption. For example, if there is an express provision in the contract stating that the parties do not intend to create legal relations, then there is no enforceable contract. This was certainly illustrated in the case of *Rose and Frank Co v Crompton Bros Ltd.*[7] In this case, the defendants were paper manufacturers. By agreement, the plaintiffs were to act as sole agents for the sale of the defendants' paper in the United States. There was also a term within the agreement which stated that it would not be subject to the legal jurisdiction of the courts, but was merely a record of the purpose and intention of the parties. When a dispute arose, the court held that, because of this clause, the contract was not binding.[8]

2.1 Mere puffs

Mere puffs are statements made in advertisements by tradesmen that may be vague or slightly exaggerated. These statements do not generally signify an intention to be legally bound. However, there are instances where specific pledges may create an intention. For example, in *Carlill v Carbolic*

[6] [1955] 3 All ER 10.
[7] [1925] AC 445.
[8] See also *Edwards v Skyways* [1964] 1 All ER 494.

Smoke Ball Co,[9] the defendant promising to give money to members of the public who contracted influenza after using their smoke ball may have indicated an intention to create legal relations.

A statement made in jest also cannot be presumed to create legal relations. Thus, if a parent jokingly says that she is selling her children for K10 each, the chances are that the courts will not consider such a statement as seriously meant.[10] This point is illustrated in *Weeks v Tybald*.[11] In this case, the defendant stated that he would give £100 to any man that would marry his daughter. The court held: 'It is not reasonable that the defendant should be bound by such general words spoken to excite suitors.'

2.2 Letters of comfort or intent

A letter of comfort is a document given by a third party to a creditor, stating that they would ensure that the debtor will meet their obligations to the creditor. Depending on the terms, these may actually be binding. The case of *Kleinwort Benson v Malaysia Mining Corp*[12] involved the plaintiff bank making an agreement to lend money to a subsidiary of the defendants. As part of the agreement, the defendants gave the plaintiff a letter assuring it that it was the defendants' policy to ensure that the business of their subsidiary was at all times in a position to meet its liabilities.

When the subsidiary went into liquidation, the plaintiff sued the defendants. The court held that the letter sent by the defendants, which was a letter of comfort, was merely a statement of the defendants' (at the time) present policy, not a promise as to a future contract. Consequently, there was no intention to create legal relations, although there was a moral responsibility on the part of the defendants to meet the debt of their liquidated subsidiary.

Letters of intent are an indication that one party is likely to enter into a contract with another party but is not ready to be bound. If the language of such a letter does not negate contractual intention, the courts may hold that the defendant is legally bound. This is especially the case where the parties act on the document for an extensive period or spend large amounts of money in reliance of the document.[13]

---

[9] [1893] 1 QB 256.

[10] In any case this might amount to slavery, which is illegal, and the contract would therefore be void—but we digress.

[11] (1605) Noy 11.

[12] [1989] 1 All ER 785.

[13] *Turriff Construction v Regalia Knitting Mills* (1971) 22 EG 169.

2.3 Free gifts

In *Esso Petroleum Co Ltd v Customs and Excise Commissioners*,[14] Esso had devised a sales promotion scheme which involved the distribution of coins bearing images of English football players to petrol stations which sold Esso petrol. The purpose of this scheme was to encourage motorists to purchase Esso petrol by giving away one coin for every four gallons of petrol purchased. The coins themselves were of little intrinsic value. However, the idea was that motorists would keep buying Esso petrol in the hope of collecting the full set of 30 coins.

The scheme was advertised by Esso in the press and on television using phrases like 'Going free, at your Esso Action Station now' and 'We are giving you a coin with every four gallons of Esso petrol you buy'. Moreover, the folders that were circulated by Esso to petrol stations contained statements like 'One coin should be given to every motorist who buys four gallons of petrol—two coins for eight gallons and so on'.

This scheme was joined by several petrol stations. The Customs and Excise Commissioners claimed that because the coins were 'produced in quantity for general sale', they were susceptible to tax.

The court held that there was an intention to create legal relations. This was owing to the fact that the coins were offered in a commercial context, which raised the presumption that they did intend to be bound.

[14] [1976] 1 WLR 1.

Chapter 5

TERMS OF THE CONTRACT

Contracts consist of various terms, which may be express or implied. Whatever the case, they determine the rights and obligations of the parties to the contract. Both express and implied terms will be covered in this chapter. In addition, this chapter will look at exclusion clauses and the doctrine of privity of contract.

1 EXPRESS TERMS

Express terms are those which are specifically agreed on by the parties. In the event that there is an express term in the contract, the courts will generally uphold it. This is illustrated in the case of *The State Lotteries Board of Zambia v Alice Tembo*.[1] In this case, Alice Tembo had purchased a lottery ticket. However, because of the negligence of the collector employed by the appellant, the ticket was not in the appropriate place. Therefore, despite the fact that she had correctly predicted the winning numbers, the appellant refused to pay out the K40 000 jackpot on offer that week.

This was because the lottery was governed by a set of conditions printed at the back of the ticket and by the rules contained within a statutory instrument. Particularly, rule 12(6) of the Pick-a-Lot Draw Rules stated as follows:

> No prize shall be paid unless the Director is satisfied that the original ticket was lodged within the designated security area at the state lottery head office, Cairo Road, Lusaka, before the draw to which the ticket relates was conducted.

The purpose behind this rule was to avert the possibility of fraudulent claims being made. Although the Supreme Court sympathised with Alice Tembo, they found in favour of the appellant.

2 THE PAROL EVIDENCE RULE

From the preceding section, it is clear what happens when there is an express written term in a contract. What happens, however, when a contract is partly written and partly oral? This is governed by the parol evidence

[1] (1988–1989) ZR 16.

rule. This rule espouses that 'evidence cannot be admitted (or, even if admitted, cannot be used) to add to or vary or contradict a written instrument'.[2]

2.1 Exceptions to the parol evidence rule

2.1.1 *Where the written agreement is not the whole agreement*

There are, however, exceptions to this rule. One of them is where the written agreement is not intended to express the whole agreement. This was certainly discussed in the case of *Holmes Limited v Buildwell Construction Company Ltd*,[3] where Bruce-Lyle J highlighted the general rule that where the parties have embodied the terms of their contract in a written document, extrinsic evidence will not be considered. However, extrinsic evidence may be admitted if it shows that the contract was not intended to express the whole agreement between the parties.[4]

2.1.2 *Operation of the contract*

Extrinsic evidence can also be permissible to show either that the contract has not yet come into operation or that it has since ceased to operate. In *Pym v Campbell*,[5] there was a written agreement for the sale of a share of a patent. However, the parties agreed that the contract would not be operative until the invention was approved by a third party. Oral evidence was admitted in this case.

2.1.3 *Collateral contract*

The parol evidence rule is also circumvented in situations where a party enters into a written contract on the faith of an oral promise by another. This is what is referred to as a collateral contract. This was illustrated in *City & Westminster Properties v Mudd*.[6] The defendant, who rented a store from the plaintiffs, also slept there. The plaintiffs were aware of this. At the time of renewal of the lease, the plaintiffs included a term which stated that the premises were to be used strictly for business purposes.

The defendant signed the lease, though he was assured orally that he could continue sleeping there. The court held that although this assurance opposed the terms of the lease, evidence of it was admissible to prove a

[2] Edwin Peel *Treitel on the Law of Contract* 12 ed (2007) 213. See also *Jacobs v Batavia and General Plantations Trust* [1924] 1 Ch 287.

[3] (1973) ZR 97.

[4] See also *Evans v Andrea Merzario* [1976] 2 All ER 930.

[5] (1856) 6 E & B 370.

[6] [1959] Ch 129.

collateral contract, enabling the tenant to plead a counter-claim for breach of contract.

2.2 Representations and terms

During contractual negotiations, certain statements may be made. It might be difficult to determine their precise legal effect. The courts look at four factors in determining whether a statement amounts to a term or a mere representation: timing, the importance of the statement, the reduction of terms to writing, and special knowledge or skills.

2.2.1 *Timing*

The court will consider the lapse of time between the making of the statement and the contract's conclusion. Should the interval be short, the statement is more than likely to be a term. In *Schawel v Reade*,[7] the plaintiff purchased a horse three weeks after the defendant had told him that it was in 'perfectly sound' condition. As it turned out, the horse was not fit. The court held that the statement could be deemed to be a term of the contract. This was especially owing to the fact that the defendant appeared to have had special knowledge about horses.[8]

2.2.2 *Importance of the statement*

Another factor that the courts will examine is whether the statement made was a pivotal factor in determining the finalisation of the contract. In *Bannerman v White*,[9] the seller of hops assured the buyer that sulphur had not been used in their cultivation. The buyer had previously stated that he would not even bother to ask the price if it had. The court held that the assurance was of such importance that, without it, the buyer would not have contracted; therefore, it was a condition of the contract.

2.2.3 *Reduction of terms to writing*

If the terms have been reduced to writing, this will also be considered by the court. In *Routledge v McKay*,[10] an action was brought for breach of an oral warranty on the sale of a motorcycle. The seller contended, inter alia,

---

[7] [1913] 2 IR 64.

[8] For a contrasting case, see *Routledge v McKay* [1954] 1 WLR 615, where the defendant stated that the motorcycle he was selling was a 1942 model. No mention was made of the date of the model when the contract itself was being signed. The court held that the lapse of a week between the two events meant that the statement could not be regarded as a contractual term.

[9] (1861) CB (NS) 844.

[10] [1954] 1 WLR 615.

that a written agreement which made no mention of the date of the model excluded the oral warranty. The Court of Appeal held that the parties' intention was recorded in the written statement. It would be inconsistent with the written agreement to hold that there was an intention to make the prior statement a contractual term.

2.2.4 *Special knowledge or skills*

Special knowledge or skills will also be a consideration. In *Harling v Eddy*,[11] the plaintiffs purchased a heifer belonging to the defendant. At the time of auction, it appeared to be rather unimpressive. The plaintiffs nonetheless proceeded with the purchase, after the defendant had represented that nothing was wrong with the animal.

As it turned out, the heifer yielded little milk and had tuberculosis, from which it died four months later. The Court of Appeal held that the statement was a term of the contract, because the vendor was in a special position to know the heifer's condition.

In *Oscar Chess v Williams*[12] the defendant, a private seller, honestly believed the car he was selling to the plaintiff was a 1948 model and described it as such. He obtained £290 in part-exchange on this basis. The car turned out to be a 1939 model. Unknown to both the buyer and the seller, the registration book had been altered, fraudulently, by the previous owner. Had the plaintiff been aware that the car was a 1939 model, they still would have been prepared to buy the car, albeit at a lower price. The Court of Appeal held that the defendant's statement was not a term of the contract.

This can be contrasted with *Dick Bentley Productions v Harold Smith Motors*,[13] where a car dealer had made a statement to a private purchaser that the car had done 20 000 miles since it had been fitted with a replacement engine and gearbox. This was in fact untrue: the car had done nearly 100 000 miles since. The Court of Appeal held that the plaintiff was entitled to damages as the representation amounted to a warranty, and the inference of a warranty was not, in the present case, rebutted. Lord Denning MR distinguished this case from *Oscar Chess v Williams*. In his view, the car dealer was clearly in a better position than the buyer to know whether the representation was in fact correct.

[11] [1951] 2 KB 739.
[12] [1975] 1 WLR 370.
[13] [1965] 2 All ER 65.

2.3 Conditions and warranties

2.3.1 *Conditions*

A condition is a major term of a contract which is vital to its main purpose, breach of which entitles the injured party to repudiate the contract. For example, in *Poussard v Spiers*,[14] the plaintiff was contracted to appear in an opera from start to finish three months later. The plaintiff fell ill, which forced the producers to engage a substitute.

A week later, the plaintiff recovered and offered to take the substitute's place. However, the defendants refused to take her back. The court held that the defendants were justified in their refusal and therefore not liable for damages. The obligation to perform from the very first night was a term of the contract. Failure to uphold this term entitled the defendants to repudiate the contract.

2.3.2 *Warranties*

A warranty, on the other hand, does not go to the root of the contract. Therefore, it is a less important term. Breach of a warranty simply gives the injured party the right to claim damages. The injured party cannot repudiate the contract on the basis of a breach of warranty.

In *Bettini v Gye*,[15] the plaintiff was engaged to perform in a season of concerts by the defendants. He undertook that he would be in London at least six days before the first concert in order to rehearse. However, he fell ill and arrived three days late. Consequently, the defendants refused to accept his services. The court held that the defendants could not repudiate the contract. The plaintiff had been engaged to perform for a reasonable period of time. The rehearsal period constituted but a scintilla of this timeframe. In this instance there was only a breach of warranty, which did not permit repudiation of the contract.

2.3.3 *Intermediate terms*

When we are dealing with intermediate terms, the injured party's right to repudiate the contract depends on the nature and consequences of the actual breach of contract.

In *Hong Kong Fir Shipping Co v Kawasaki Kisen Kaisha*,[16] it was mutually agreed that the defendants would charter a vessel for a period of 24 months, 'she being fitted in every way for ordinary cargo service', and

[14] (1876) 1 QBD 410.
[15] (1876) 1 QBD 183.
[16] [1962] 2 QB 26.

that the owners would 'maintain her in a thoroughly efficient state in hull and machinery during service'.

When the vessel was delivered to the charterers, her engine-room was undermanned and her engine-room staff was incompetent. During the voyage, the vessel was off hire for repairs to her engines for a total period of about five weeks. At another point in the voyage, it was found that the engines were in a very bad state and it would take a further 15 weeks to make the vessel seaworthy. By the time it became seaworthy, the vessel was available to the defendants for 17 months. The defendants wrote to the owners to repudiate the contract, claiming that the term as to seaworthiness was a condition of the contract. Any breach thus entitled them to repudiate the contract. The plaintiffs brought an action for wrongful repudiation. The court held that the charterers were not entitled to repudiate the contract. The test here was whether the injured party was deprived substantially of the whole benefit they intended on deriving from the contract.

In *Mihalis Angelos*,[17] the owners of a ship let it to charterers. They promised that the ship would be ready to load around 1 July and would proceed to a certain port for the loading of cargo. Further, the charterer would have the option of cancelling the charter if the ship was not ready by 20 July.

The charterer, unable to get cargo by 17 July, cancelled the charter. He alleged that it was frustrated. The ship itself was not ready until 23 July. At trial it was argued that the charterer was entitled to avoid the contract on 17 July. This was because of a breach of contract by the shipowner. That is to say, there was an implied promise that there were reasonable grounds for believing that the ship would be ready on 1 July. The trial judge held that there was a breach of this term. However, the term was not a condition, and the breach was not so fundamental as to give right to terminate the contract. The Court of Appeal held that the term was a condition and that the charterer had properly avoided the contract, though on wrongful grounds.

In *Bunge Corporation v Tradax Export*,[18] there was a contract for the sale and purchase of soya bean meal. It was agreed that a shipment was to be made by 30 June. The contract provided that the buyers had to provide a vessel and to give at least 15 days' notice of its probable readiness. Such notice was rendered on 17 June, which was less than 15 days before the end of the shipment period. The seller argued a breach and sought to repudiate

[17] [1971] 1 QB 164.
[18] [1981] 1 WLR 71.

the contract. The House of Lords held that this was a condition, which entitled the sellers to repudiate the contract.

The case of *Schuler v Wickman Machine Tools*[19] concerned an agency contract in which Wickman were the exclusive selling agents in the UK for Schuler's goods. A condition was that the distributor should visit six named customers once a week to solicit orders. By clause 11 of the contract, either party could determine the contract if the other committed 'a material breach' of its obligations. Wickman committed some minor breaches of this term, and Schuler terminated the agreement. The court held that it was not the intention of the parties that Schuler should have the right to terminate the agreement if Wickman failed to meet one of the obliged number of visits.

3 IMPLIED TERMS

There are situations in which terms may not be expressed in the contract. However, they may be implied into the contract either by custom, by the court or by statute.

3.1 Terms implied by custom

Contractual terms may be implied into the contract by custom. This was established in *Hutton v Warren*,[20] where a landlord had given a tenant six months' notice to quit. The landlord also insisted that the tenant continue to cultivate the land during the notice period as provided by custom. The tenant successfully argued that the same custom entitled him to fair allowance for the seeds and labour he had used on the land. Although the lease was silent on this, the court held that the custom would be implied into the lease. The court thus found for the tenant.

3.2 Terms implied by the court

There are two means through which the court may imply a term into a contract. The first is through terms implied by fact and the other is through terms implied in law.

3.2.1 *Intention of the parties or terms implied by fact*

Terms are implied by fact when the court is satisfied that the parties must have intended a certain provision as a matter of fact to be part of the agreement, despite them having omitted to insert it into the contract.

[19] [1974] AC 235.
[20] (1936) 1 M & W 466.

In *The Moorcock*,[21] the defendants were owners of a wharf used by the plaintiffs for mooring facilities for their ship, which was called 'The Moorcock'. The ship was damaged after hitting a rock at low tide. The defendants had no legal control of the river bed, but could have ascertained its state had they attempted to do so. The court held that it there was an implied obligation on the wharf owners that the wharf be reasonably safe for the ship and that they had breached this obligation.

A more recently applied test is referred to as the 'officious bystander test', which was propounded in *Shirlaw v Southern Foundries*.[22] If a bystander were to suggest some express provision and both parties would respond 'oh, of course', then the term is binding. If they would not, the parties could not possibly be bound by the term.[23]

3.2.2 *Relationship between the parties or terms implied by law*

Terms implied by fact simply act as a gap filler. On the other hand, terms implied by law are those attached to particular types of contract by the law itself. In the case of *Liverpool City Council v Irwin*,[24] the plaintiffs, who were tenants in the defendants' tower block, brought an action alleging that the defendants had breached an implied covenant for quiet enjoyment when the tower block was in disuse in the following areas: there were defects in the stairs and lifts, and internal rubbish chutes became blocked. The court held that the defendants were in breach of this implied covenant.

3.3 Terms implied by statute

Acts of Parliament and statutory instruments also have, over the years, implied terms into particular types of contract. The Sale of Goods Act 1893 is an example of a statute that implies terms into a contract. For example, section 12 of the Sale of Goods Act provides that it is implied that when a seller is making a sale, they have the right to do so, and further that the buyer has the right to quiet enjoyment of the goods. There are other examples of implied terms found in sections 13 to 15 of that Act.

4 EXCLUSION AND LIMITING CLAUSES

Exclusion clauses are terms which are inserted into a contract with the aim of excluding or limiting the liability of one party for negligence or breach

[21] (1889) 14 PD 64.
[22] [1940] AC 701.
[23] See *Wilson v Best Travel* [1993] 1 All ER 353.
[24] [1977] AC 239.

of contract. Such a clause only applies if it is incorporated into the contract. Further, the clause must extend to the loss in question.

4.1 Incorporation

4.1.1 *Signed documents*

Once the plaintiff signs a document containing an exclusion clause, they are automatically bound by its terms. The case of *L'Estrange v Graucob*[25] propounded that this is the case even where the party has not had a chance to ascertain what the contract says.[26]

In the case of *Curtis v Chemical Cleaning Co*,[27] the plaintiff took a wedding dress to the defendant cleaning company. After being told by the assistant that it exempted the cleaners from liability for damage to beads and sequins, the plaintiff signed a piece of paper headed 'Receipt'. In actual fact, the said receipt had an exclusion clause excluding liability 'for any damage however arising'.

When the dress was returned it was badly stained. The court held that the cleaners could not escape liability for damage to the material of the dress by relying on the exemption clause. This was owing to the fact that the scope of the exclusion clause had been misrepresented by the defendant's assistant.

4.1.2 *Unsigned documents*

Exclusion clauses must be contained in a document that the party would assume contains contractual terms. It should not be contained in a document that merely acknowledges payment, for example, a receipt. In *Parker v South Eastern Railway Co*,[28] the plaintiff had deposited a bag in a cloakroom at the defendant's railway station. He was given a paper ticket which simply read 'See Back'. Behind this paper ticket were several terms. One of those terms stated: 'The company will not be responsible for any package exceeding the value of £10.' When the plaintiff's bag went missing, he claimed a sum of £24.10sh. The defendant company said they were immunised from liability by the exclusion clause.

The court held that they could not rely on the clause. This is because the reasonable person would assume that the ticket was merely a receipt rather

[25] [1934] 2 KB 394.

[26] Scrutton LJ opined: 'When a document containing contractual terms is signed, then, in the absence of fraud, or, I will add, misrepresentation, the party signing it is bound, and it is wholly immaterial whether he has read the document or not.'

[27] [1951] 1 KB 805.

[28] (1877) 2 CPD 416.

than a document containing contractual terms. Therefore, the exclusion clause had not been incorporated.

Similarly, in *Chappleton v Barry UDC*,[29] the defendant council provided deck chairs on the beach. They were stacked up on the beach, and next to them was a notice. The plaintiff received two such chairs from the attendant but did not read the notice. Upon payment of the fee, two tickets were given to him, but he did not read them. He just put them in his pocket. At the back of the tickets were the following printed words: 'The Council will not be liable for any accident or damage arising from hire of chair.'

The plaintiff was injured when a deck chair collapsed. The Court of Appeal held that the plaintiff was entitled to recover damages in respect of his injuries. This is because the ticket was a mere receipt and its object was simply to act as proof that a hirer had in fact paid for the ticket and to show them how long they could use the chair.

In *Olley v Marlborough Court*,[30] the plaintiff was a guest at the defendant hotel. She left the room for a few hours, locking the door of her room and leaving the key on the rack at the reception office. Upon her return, she discovered that the key was missing and some of her belongings had been stolen from her room.

The hotel argued that the plaintiff was subject to the terms contained on a notice exhibited in her room. The said notice stated: 'The proprietors will not hold themselves responsible for articles lost or stolen unless handed to the manageress for safe custody.'

The plaintiff brought an action for negligence. The court held that the notice had not been incorporated into the contract between the plaintiff and the defendant. This is because the contract was made in the hall of the hotel, before the plaintiff had entered her bedroom and before she had been afforded an opportunity to see the notice.

From this, we can see that reasonably sufficient notice of the clause must be given to the party. What is reasonable, however, is really a question of fact. It will thus depend on the circumstances of the case. This was shown in the case of *Thornton v Shoe Lane Parking*,[31] where the defendant ran a system at their car park where an automatic machine issued tickets. The plaintiff was issued one such ticket and it stated that it was issued subject to conditions displayed inside the car park.

The conditions inside the car park were in small print; one of them

[29] [1940] 1 KB 532.
[30] [1949] 1 KB 532.
[31] [1971] 2 QB 163.

excluded liability for damages to vehicles or injury to customers. The plaintiff was injured partly due to the defendant's negligence. The court held that the plaintiff was not bound by the ostensible exclusion clause because it had not been incorporated. In the court's view, they could not hold anyone bound 'unless it is drawn to his attention in the most explicit way'.[32]

4.2 Previous dealings

As the case of *Spurling v Bradshaw*[33] illustrates, an exclusion clause may be incorporated into the contract where there has been a previous course of dealings between the parties on the same terms. In this case, the defendant had purchased eight barrels of orange juice and sent them to the plaintiff for storage. A few days later, the defendant received a document from the plaintiff acknowledging receipt of the barrels. The document also contained the following clause:

> We will not in any circumstances when acting either as warehousemen . . . or in any other capacity, be liable for any loss, damage or detention howsoever, whensoever, or wheresoever occasioned in respect of any goods entrusted to or carried or handled by us in the course of our business, even when such loss, damage or detention may have been occasioned by the negligence, wrongful act or default of ourselves or our servants or agents.

When the defendant collected the barrels, some were empty and some contained dirty water. The defendant refused to pay the storage charges and was sued by the plaintiff. The court held that although the defendant did not receive the document containing the exclusion clause until after the conclusion of the contract, the clause had been incorporated in the contract. This is because the parties had engaged in regular business dealings over the years. The defendant had received similar documents on previous occasions. As such he was now bound by the terms contained in them.

A contrasting case is *Hollier v Rambler Motors*,[34] where the plaintiff had used the defendants' garage three or four times. On some occasions he would sign a contract that excluded the defendants from liability for damage by fire. On this occasion no such document was signed, and the plaintiff's car was badly damaged in a fire. The court held that there was no regular course of dealing here. Therefore, the defendants were liable.[35]

---

[32] See also *Interfoto v Stiletto Ltd* [1989] QB 433.
[33] [1956] 2 All ER 121.
[34] [1972] 2 AB 71.
[35] *British Crane Hire v Ipswich Plant Hire* [1974] QB 303.

4.3 Privity of contract

The doctrine of privity of contract means that a person who is not a party to a contract (a third party) is not protected by an exclusion clause in that contract. This is so even though the clauses purportedly extend to the third party.[36] Thus, in the case of *Scruttons v Midlands Silicones*,[37] the House of Lords held that a limiting clause did not apply to the defendants because they were not parties to the contract. In essence, this case concerned a contract to ship a drum, which was concluded by a shipping company and the plaintiff. It limited the liability of the shipping company to £179 per package. The defendants were hired by the shipping company to upload the drum. In the process they damaged it through their negligence. The plaintiff brought an action to the full extent of the damage, which was £593.

4.4 Collateral contracts

An exclusion clause will not be deemed incorporated if it is inserted in a collateral contract. This is illustrated in *Andrews v Hopkinson*.[38] The plaintiff here was interested in purchasing the defendant's car, and was assured by the defendant that it was 'a good little bus. I would stake my life on it'. An agreement was drawn up whereby the plaintiff was to buy the car by a way of a hire-purchase arrangement with a finance company. The car was delivered to the plaintiff, who signed a note to the effect that he was satisfied with its condition, which action precluded the plaintiff from suing the finance company. The court held that the defendant was liable because there was a collateral contract in which the defendant promised that the car was in good condition and the plaintiff promised to enter into the hire-purchase agreement.

4.5 The battle of the forms

As a general rule, when there is a 'battle of the forms', the contract will be made on the last set of terms sent. In *British Road Services v Arthur Crutchley Ltd*,[39] Arthur Crutchley had received whisky from the British Road Services at their warehouse. The delivery note contained the British Road Services' conditions. Arthur Crutchley stamped the delivery note 'Received under AC's conditions'. The whisky was stolen, and it was held that Arthur Crutchley's conditions applied. This was owing to the fact that

[36] See *Adler v Dickinson* [1954] 3 All ER 396.
[37] [1962] AC 446.
[38] [1957] 1 QB 229.
[39] [1968] 1 All ER 811.

the stamp was a counter-offer, which was accepted by the British Road Services when they handed over the whisky.

4.6 Interpretation

The wording of the exclusion clause must extend to the damage that the defendant wishes to insulate themselves from. The Supreme Court of Zambia highlighted this in the case of *Zambia Horticultural Products Ltd v Tembo*.[40] Here, the appellants agreed to store chickens for the respondent in their cold room. However, the temperature of the room was not low enough. Consequently, the chickens went bad and the respondent sued.

The appellants in response produced a letter that contained a clause stating that 'the company will bear no responsibilities on the condition of the commodities stored in the cold room by yourselves'. Therefore they argued that the terms of the letter exempted the appellants from liability by negligence. The Supreme Court held that, since there was no express reference to negligence, the court would have to consider whether the words used were wide enough in their ordinary meaning to cover negligence. The wording in this case could not cover negligence, and the appellants could therefore not rely on the exclusion clause to avoid liability.

Similarly, in *AMI Zambia Ltd v Chibuye*,[41] the appellant, among other things, stored goods for customers. The respondent's goods were stored with the appellant, and some of those goods were subsequently stolen. The appellant sought to rely on an exclusion clause which said that goods would be stored 'at owner's risk'. Ngulube CJ stated:

> In the case at hand, there was no suggestion that the clause 'at owner's risk' had been given a definition in the contract so that it would have been necessary to ascertain its meaning, like any other clause in a contract, having regard to the nature and purpose of the contract, and the context within which the words were used.

The Supreme Court was not persuaded, on the facts, that the appellant could have an exemption from their own wrongdoing by the misconduct of their staff. The words, in essence, were not wide enough.[42]

4.7 The 'main purpose' rule

If the exemption clause is incongruous with the main purpose of the contract, then it may be struck out by the courts. The case of *Glynn v Margetson*[43] is instructive in this regard. The defendants had been

[40] (1988–1989) ZR 214.
[41] SCZ Judgment 8 of 1999.
[42] *George Kakoma v The State Lotteries Board of Zambia* (1981) ZR 111.
[43] [1893] AC 351.

contracted to deliver oranges from Malaga to Liverpool on a contract that allowed the ship to call at any port from Africa to Europe.

The ship sailed some 355 miles east of Malaga to pick up other cargo before proceeding to Liverpool. On arrival at Liverpool, it was held that the oranges had gone bad, and the defendants attempted to rely on the exclusion. It was held that the main purpose of the contract was to deliver the oranges and, due to the wide wording of the exclusion, that it be construed to refer only to ports on the way from Malaga to Liverpool. The defendants were therefore liable.[44]

4.8 The doctrine of fundamental breach

The traditional position in common law was that a fundamental breach could not be excluded or restricted in any circumstances. However, this rule was later rejected on the basis that it militated against freedom of contract in *UGS Finance v National Mortgage Bank of* Greece,[45] which was unanimously approved by the House of Lords in *Suisse Atlantique*[46] and *Photo Production Ltd v Securicor Transport*.[47]

5 THE DOCTRINE OF PRIVITY

5.1 Introduction

As Treitel succinctly puts it, the 'doctrine of privity means that a contract cannot, as a general rule, confer rights or impose obligations arising under it on any person except the parties to it'.[48] This is because the only person that can enforce a promise is the promisee. Therefore, if a third party is not a promisee, then they are not privy to the contract.[49]

In addition to this, there is the principle that consideration must move from the promisee. Thus, in *Tweddle v Atkinson*,[50] C could not sue for an

---

[44] See also *Evans Ltd v Andrea Merzario Ltd* [1976] 1 WLR 1078, where the plaintiffs had for many years imported machines from Italy. They employed the services of the defendants for precisely this purpose. The defendants made an oral promise to the plaintiffs that the goods of the latter would continue to be stowed below deck. On one occasion, the plaintiffs' container was stored on deck, and was lost when it slid overboard. The Court of Appeal held that the defendants could not rely on an exemption clause contained in the standard conditions of the forwarding trade, on which the parties had contracted, because it was incongruous to the oral promise that had been given. The oral assurance that goods would be carried inside the ship superseded the written exclusion clause.

[45] [1964] 1 Lloyd's Rep 446.

[46] [1967] 1 AC 361.

[47] [1980] AC 827.

[48] Peel n 2, 616.

[49] See *Dunlop Tyre Co v Selfridge* [1915] AC 847. where Lord Haldane stated that 'only a person who is a party to a contract can sue on it'.

[50] (1861) 1 B & S 393.

amount owed to him by A's estate, because he was not party to the agreement and, as Wightman J said, 'no stranger to the consideration can take advantage of the of the contract though made for his benefit'.

5.2 Exceptions

5.2.1 *Collateral contracts*

If there is a contract between the two parties accompanied by a collateral contract between one of them and a third party, this may be binding. In the case of *Shanklin Pier v Detel Products*,[51] the plaintiff, Shanklin, had entered into a contract with A to paint a pier. Shanklin had asked A to use paint made by Detel, which, by guarantee, lasted seven years. The paint lasted three months and therefore Shanklin brought an action against Detel. This action succeeded on the ground that the plaintiff could sue on a collateral contract.

5.2.2 *Agency*

Another exception to the doctrine of privity is that of agency. Under an agency agreement, the agent is able to sue on behalf of their principal. Further, an agent can form a binding contract between the principal and a third party. In *Scruttons* a drum of chemicals had been shipped to the plaintiff consignees on a ship belonging to the carrier United States Inc.

The bill of lading stated that the carrier's liability for damage was limited to $500 per package. The defendants were engaged to discharge the carrier's vessel and act as agents in the delivery of the goods to the consignees, by a contract that limited their liability to $500. The defendants negligently dropped the drum, causing damage worth $593, and the plaintiffs subsequently brought an action claiming $593. It was held that the defendants could rely on the exclusion clause because they were agents. Therefore they were liable only for $500.

[51] [1951] 2 KB 854.

Chapter 6

MISREPRESENTATION

A misrepresentation occurs when one party makes a false statement of fact to another which, although not a term of the contract, induces the other party to enter it. Misrepresentation is a ground on which the innocent party may rescind the contract or claim damages, or even both.

1 FALSE STATEMENT OF FACT

1.1 Statements of opinion

A false statement of opinion does not generally constitute a misrepresentation of fact. This was espoused in the case of *Bisset v Wilkinson*,[1] where Sim J opined:

> In ordinary circumstances, any statement made by an owner who has been occupying his own farm as to its carrying capacity would be regarded as a statement of fact. . . . This, however, is not such a case. . . . In these circumstances . . . the defendants were not justified in regarding anything said by the plaintiff as to the carrying capacity as being anything more than an expression of his opinion on the subject.

The plaintiff in this case had acquired land for the purpose of sheep farming from the defendant. The defendant during negotiations purported that the land would carry 2 000 sheep. On this basis the plaintiff purchased the property, although both parties were well aware that the defendant had not carried on sheep farming on the land.

Sim J's view was accepted by the Privy Council. It held that the purchaser had no right to rescind the contract:

> Since an erroneous opinion stated by the party affirming the contract, though it may have been relied upon and have induced the contract on the part of the party who seeks rescission, gives no title to relief unless fraud is established . . . If a reasonable man with the vendor's knowledge could not have come to the conclusion he stated, the description of that conclusion as an opinion would not necessarily protect him against rescission for misrepresentation, but what was actually the capacity in competent hands of the land the purchasers purchased had never been and never was practically ascertained.

However, the case of *Smith v Land & House Property Corp*[2] illustrates that in an instance where the person giving the statement was in a position to

[1] [1927] AC 177.
[2] (1884) 28 Ch D 7.

know the true facts and it can be proven that they could not have reasonably held such an opinion as a result, such an opinion can be treated as a statement of fact.

In the *Smith* case, the defendants agreed to purchase the plaintiff's hotel, which was advertised as being let to a 'most desirable tenant'. It turned out, however, that the tenant was bankrupt, and the defendants as a result refused to complete the contract. The plaintiff sued for specific performance. The Court of Appeal held that the plaintiff's statement was a fact and not a matter of mere opinion.

If the statement is a mere puff, this does not constitute a representation. This was propounded in the case of *Dimmock v Hallet*,[3] where the court held that the description of land as 'fertile and improvable' was not a representation.

1.2 Statements as to the future

When the defendant makes a statement as to what they will do in the future, this does not constitute a misrepresentation *per se*. However, if the defendant knows that this promise will not be carried out, they may be liable if that promise has induced another person to enter into the contract.

In *Edgington v Fitzmaurice*,[4] the plaintiff was induced to take debentures in a company because of, as alleged, a misstatement in the prospectus which was framed in such a way as to lead to the belief that the debentures would be a charge on the property of the company, and that the loans were to pay off pressing liabilities of the company—not to complete alterations on valuable property acquired. The plaintiff claimed repayment on the ground that money was obtained from him through fraudulent misstatements.

The Court of Appeal held that the statement rendered by the defendant amounted to a statement of fact. Therefore, it amounted to a misrepresentation. The plaintiff was thus entitled to rescind the contract. The court observed that the state of someone's mind is 'as much a fact as the state of his digestion'. It is, of course, difficult to prove what the state of someone's mind is at a particular time. However, if it can be ascertained, then it is as much a fact as anything else. Thus, a misrepresentation as to the state of someone's mind amounts to a misstatement of fact.[5]

[3] (1866) 2 Ch App 21.
[4] (1885) 29 Ch D 459.
[5] See also *Esso Petroleum v Mardon* [1976] QB 801.

1.3 Statements of the law

Traditionally, a false statement of law was not regarded as actionable, because the presumption is that everyone knows the law. However, this position was eventually brought into doubt after the decision in *Kleinwort Benson Ltd v Lincoln City Council*,[6] where the House of Lords held that the rule precluding the recovery of money paid under mistake of law was no longer tenable.

This decision certainly had far-reaching implications regarding the rules on misrepresentations of the law. The issue came before the House of Lords in *Pankhania v London Borough of Hackney*,[7] where the misrepresentation in question was a statement that a company, NCP, who occupied a car park, was actually a contractual licensee, and thus their occupation was determinable on three months' notice. In fact, NCP was a business tenant with security of tenure. The judge held that the misrepresentation in this case was actionable. The judge opined:

> I have concluded that the 'misrepresentation of law' rule has not survived the decision in *Kleinwort Benson Ltd v Lincoln City Council* . . . [i]ts historical origin is an off-shoot of the 'mistake of law' rule, created by analogy with it, and the two are logically inter-dependent. Both are grounded in the maxim 'ignorantia juris non excusat' [ignorance of the law is no excuse], a tag whose dubious utility would have been enhanced had it gone on to explain who was not excused, and from what.
>
> In *Solle v Butcher*,[8] the defendant let a flat to the plaintiff at an annual rent of £140. Thereafter, the defendant took a long lease of the building. This was with the intention of repairing bomb damage and making substantial alterations.

Due to this, the plaintiff started paying rent at £250 per year for some time, and then took proceedings for a declaration that the standard rent was £140. The defendant argued that the flat had become a new and separate dwelling by reason of change of identity. Therefore, it did not fall within the ambit of the Rent Restrictions Acts. This was held to be a mistake as to the state of the flat and not a mistake of law.

1.4 Silence

The general rule is that silence does not amount to a misrepresentation. There is no duty to disclose facts which might influence the other party's decision one way or the other.

In *Smith v Hughes*,[9] the plaintiff offered to sell oats to the defendant by way of sample. The defendant agreed to the whole quantity. However, when

6 [1999] 2 AC 349.
7 [2002] EWHC 2441.
8 [1950] 1 KB 671.
9 (1871) LR 6 QB 597.

the plaintiff delivered a portion of them, the defendant complained that the oats were new oats, whereas he thought he had contracted for old oats. New oats were of no use to him. The plaintiff refused to take them back and sued for the price. This is despite the fact that he knew the oats were new. Blackburn J opined:

> [O]n the sale of a specific article, unless there be a warranty making it part of the bargain that it possesses some particular quality, the purchaser must take the article he has bought, though it does not possess that quality. And I agree that, even if the vendor was aware that the purchaser thought that the article possessed that quality, and would not have entered into the contract unless he had so thought, still the purchaser is bound, unless the vendor was guilty of some fraud or deceit upon him. A mere abstinence from disabusing the purchaser of that impression is not fraud or deceit, for, whatever may be the case in a court of morals, there is no legal obligation on the vendor to inform the purchaser that he is under a mistake which has not been induced by the act of the vendor.

Therefore, silence does not amount to misrepresentation. However, the representor must not misleadingly tell only part of the truth. A statement that does not convey the whole truth may be regarded as a misrepresentation.[10]

In addition, where there is a change of circumstances and a statement becomes false, there is a duty on the representor to disclose the truth. Thus in *With v O'Flanagan*,[11] Lord Wright MR stated that 'if a statement has been made which is true at the time, but which during the course of negotiations becomes untrue, then the person who knows that it has become untrue is under an obligation to disclose to the other the change of circumstances'.

1.5 Contracts uberrimae fidei

Contracts of the utmost good faith impose a duty of disclosure of all material facts where one party is in a very strong position to know the truth. A material fact is one which would influence a reasonable person in making the contract; if a party fails to disclose this, the contract may be avoided.[12]

Where there is a fiduciary relationship between the parties to a contract, a duty of disclosure will arise, eg lawyer and client, bank manager and client, trustee and beneficiary, and inter-family agreements.

---

[10] *Nottingham Brick & Tile Co v Butler* (1889) 16 QBD 778.

[11] [1936] Ch 575.

[12] *Lambert v Co-Operative Insurance Society* [1975] 2 Lloyd's Rep 485.

2 THE MISREPRESENTATION MUST HAVE INDUCED THE CONTRACT

2.1 Materiality

The misrepresentation must be material: it must have induced the reasonable person to enter into the contract. The case of *Museprime Properties v Adhill Properties*[13] involved three properties, being sold by auction, which were wrongly represented in relation to their rent being open to negotiation. The statements in the auction particulars, and reiterated by the auctioneer, misrepresented the position with regard to rent reviews when, in fact, two of the three properties' rent reviews had already been triggered and new rents agreed. The plaintiff company successfully bid for the three properties. Upon discovering the true situation, the plaintiff commenced an action for rescission. The defendant company countered that the misrepresentations were not such as to induce any reasonable person to contract. The court disagreed.

This case therefore illustrates that this rule is not strictly objective. In this case, the judge took the view that any misrepresentation which induces a person to enter into a contract should be a ground for rescission of that contract. If the misrepresentation would have induced a reasonable person to enter into the contract, then the court will presume that the representee was so induced, and the onus will be on the representor to show that the representee did not rely on the misrepresentation, either wholly or in part. If, however, the misrepresentation would not have induced a reasonable person to contract, the onus will be on the representee to show that the misrepresentation induced them to act as they did.

2.2 Reliance

The representee must also have relied on the statements. It is advanced that there can be no reliance if the representee was not aware of the misrepresentation. In *Horsfall v Thomas*,[14] for example, the buyer of a defective gun had not examined it before purchasing it. The court held that the concealment of a defect in the gun did not affect his decision to purchase it. This is because he was not aware of the misrepresentation and could not have been induced by it. Therefore, his action failed.

Further, there can be no reliance where the representee relies on their own judgement rather than the misrepresentation. In *Attwood v Small*,[15] the

[13] [1990] 36 EG 114.
[14] (1862) 1 H & C 90.
[15] (1838) 6 CI & F 232.

sellers of a mine gave exaggerated statements as to its earning capacity to its would-be purchasers. The purchasers did counter-check with their own experts, but these experts erroneously reported them as correct. Six months after the sale had been completed, the purchasers found the sellers' statements to be inaccurate. Therefore, they sought to rescind the contract on account of misrepresentation. The House of Lords held that there had been no misrepresentation in this instance, because the purchasers did not rely on the representations made.[16]

3 TYPES OF MISREPRESENTATION

3.1 Fraudulent misrepresentation

The first type of misrepresentation is 'fraudulent misrepresentation'. This was defined in *Derry v Peek*[17] as a statement 'made (i) knowingly, or (ii) without belief in its truth, or (iii) recklessly, careless as to whether it be true or false'. Thus, if one makes a statement which they honestly believe to be true, then it cannot be fraudulent.

The case of *Derry v Peek* concerned a company which had applied for a special Act of Parliament authorising it to run trams by steam power. The Act was passed, and provided that the trams were to be moved by animal power or, with the consent of the Board of Trade, by steam or mechanical power. In the belief that such consent would be granted in due course, the directors of the company issued a prospectus claiming that they had the right to use steam power. Consequently, the plaintiff bought shares in the company. The Board of Trade did not grant their consent, and the company was wound up. The plaintiff brought an action for deceit. In this case the House of Lords held that the defendants were not fraudulent in this case. Although they had made a careless statement, they had earnestly believed in its truth.

3.2 Negligent misrepresentation

Negligent misrepresentation is a false statement made by a person who has no reasonable grounds for believing the statement to be true. At common

[16] See also *Redgrave v Hurd* (1881) 20 Ch D 1. Here the plaintiff, a solicitor, advertised for a partner. The defendant responded and the plaintiff represented that he was making £300 to £400 a year, which was not the case. Once the plaintiff had produced summaries, it became apparent that the plaintiff was making less than £200 a year. When the defendant queried how the difference was made up, the plaintiff showed him myriad letters and papers which, according to him, related to other business which he had done. The defendant merely glanced at the books and eventually proceeded to take a shore in the practice. The defendant discovered that the practice had no value and refused to complete the contract. The Court of Appeal gave judgment for the defendant.

[17] (1889) 14 App Cas 337.

law, damages may be recoverable in tort for negligent misstatements that cause financial loss.[18] However, the representee has to prove that a special relationship existed between the parties.

Duty will arise where there is a purely commercial relationship and the representor either has or professes to have some specialist knowledge or skill, and knows that the representee will rely on the misrepresentation.[19]

Negligent misrepresentation is also covered in section 3 of the Misrepresentation Act.[20] Section 3(1) provides that a person who enters into a contract as a result of fraudulent misrepresentation is entitled to recover damages. The representor is also liable in instances where the misrepresentation was not made fraudulently, unless they can prove that they had reasonable grounds to believe that the facts represented were true up until the contract was made.

Section 3(2) further provides that a person who is induced into entering into a contract by reason other than fraudulent misrepresentation is entitled either to rescind the contract or to damages in lieu of rescission.

4 REMEDIES FOR MISREPRESENTATION

4.1 Rescission

In *Car & Universal Finance v Caldwell*,[21] Norris had purchased a car from the defendant by way of a cheque. The cheque was dishonoured when it was presented the following day. The defendant immediately informed the police, as well as the Automobile Association, of the fraudulent transaction. Subsequently, Norris sold the car to X, who sold it to Z, who then went on to sell it to the plaintiffs. The question here was whether the defendant's conduct and representations amounted to a rescission of the initial contract of sale. The court held that the contract was voidable due to the fraudulent misrepresentation, and that the owner had done everything he could in the circumstances to avoid the contract. As it had been avoided before the sale to the third party, no title was passed to them and the owner could reclaim the car.

4.2 Bars to rescission

4.2.1 *Affirmation of the contract*

If the injured party is fully aware of the misrepresentation and of their right to rescind and still expressly states that they wish to continue with the

[18] See *Hedley Byrne v Heller* [1964] AC 465.
[19] See *Esso Petroleum v Mardon* n 5.
[20] Chapter 69 of the Laws of Zambia.
[21] [1965] 1 QB 525.

contract, then the parties are deemed to have affirmed the contract. In *Long v Lloyd*,[22] the defendant advertised the sale of a lorry that was in 'exceptional condition'. The defendant also suggested to the plaintiff that the lorry did 11 miles to the gallon, which was not the case. In fact, it did only 5 miles per gallon. In addition to this, the lorry developed faults. The plaintiff accepted the defendant's offer to pay for some of the repairs. Notwithstanding this, when the lorry set out on a longer journey, it broke down. This time the plaintiff demanded his money back and, as it turned out, the lorry had not been in a roadworthy condition from the outset. However, the defendant's representations concerning it had been honestly made. The Court of Appeal held that the plaintiff was not entitled to rescind the contract because he had accepted the lorry as it was before he purported to rescind. The second journey amounted, in the court's view, to an affirmation of the contract.

4.2.2 *Lapse of time*

If a reasonable period has elapsed and the injured party has not taken an action to rescind the contract, then the right to rescission is lost. In instances of fraudulent misrepresentation, the clock starts to tick once the fraud has been discovered. When it comes to non-fraudulent misrepresentation, on the other hand, time starts running after the date of the contract.

In *Leaf v International Galleries*,[23] the plaintiff had purchased a picture from the defendant. The defendant had incorrectly represented it to have been painted by 'J Constable' when it had not. The plaintiff did not discover this until five years later and claimed rescission immediately. The Court of Appeal held that the plaintiff had lost his right to rescission after such a long period of time. The only remedy available after such a period was for damages, a claim the plaintiff had not brought before the court.

4.2.3 *Restitution in integrum impossible*

In the event that the parties cannot be restored to their original position, the injured party does not have the right to rescind. Thus in *Vigers v Pike*,[24] the representee could not rescind a lease of a mine which had been entered into as a result of a misrepresentation, because there had been considerable extraction of minerals since the contract had been entered into.

However, in the event that substantial restoration is possible, the remedy

[22] [1958] 1 WLR 753.
[23] [1950] 2 KB 86.
[24] (1842) 8 Cl & F 562.

is still available. In *Armstrong v Jackson*,[25] a stockbroker was instructed by a client to buy 600 shares in a certain company. The stockbroker did not buy these from the open market, but instead sold his own shares in the company. Here the court held that the client could rescind the contract. This was on account of the broker's breach of duty. He still had the identical shares and was able to return them, together with the dividends he had received.

4.3 Indemnity

The courts may also order an indemnity, which is a payment of money to the representee by the representor for expenses necessarily accrued in complying with the terms of the contract. The case of *Whittington v Seale-Hayne*[26] involved breeders of prize poultry. They were induced to take a lease of certain property belonging to the defendants by an oral representation that the premises were in a sanitary condition.

This representation was not contained in the lease. Therefore, it was not a term of the contract. It later turned out that the water supply was in fact poisoned. The manager fell ill and the stock died. The terms of the lease demanded that the plaintiffs pay rent to the defendants and rates to the local authority. They were also required to make certain repairs as ordered by the council. The court rescinded the lease and also held that the plaintiffs could recover the rents, rates and repairs under the covenants in the lease, but nothing more.

4.4 Damages

4.4.1 *Fraudulent misrepresentation*

The case of *Doyle v Olby (Ironmongers) Ltd*[27] involved the purchase of an ironmonger's business. Things subsequently turned out markedly different to what the vendors had led the plaintiff to believe. The plaintiff was awarded damages for fraudulent misrepresentation. The appeal was advanced in relation to, among other issues, the measure of damages. Lord Denning MR stated:

> In contract, the damages are limited to what may reasonably be supposed to have been in the contemplation of the parties. In fraud, they are not so limited. The defendant is bound to make reparation for all the actual damage directly flowing from the fraudulent inducement. The person who has been defrauded is entitled to say: 'I would not have

[25] [1917] 2 KB 822.
[26] (1900) 82 LT 49.
[27] [1969] 2 QB 158.

> entered into this bargain at all but for your representation. Owing to your fraud, I have not only lost all the money I paid to you, but, what is more, I have been put to a large amount of extra expense as well and suffered this or that extra damages.' All such damages can be recovered: and it does not lie in the mouth of the fraudulent person to say that they could not reasonably have been foreseen.

Damages may include costs for lost opportunities.[28] However, the plaintiff is not entitled to damages in situations where they discovered the misrepresentation and had an opportunity to avoid further losses.[29]

4.4.2 *Negligent misrepresentation*

The injured party may claim damages for negligent misrepresentation at common law. However, they may only recover for losses that are reasonably foreseeable.[30] They may also claim damages for misrepresentation under section 3(1) of the Misrepresentation Act.

4.4.3 *Wholly innocent misrepresentation*

The plaintiff may be entitled to rescind the contract even where the misrepresentation has been made 'otherwise than fraudulently'. They may also be entitled to damages in lieu of rescission.

5 EXCLUDING LIABILITY FOR MISREPRESENTATION

Statutory law indicates that it is impossible to exclude liability for misrepresentation. This is certainly provided for in section 4 of the Misrepresentation Act. It provides that any agreement which contains a provision which excludes or restricts any liability for misrepresentation has no effect in contract law.

---

[28] *East v Maurer* [1991] 2 All ER 733.
[29] *Downs v Chappell* [1996] 3 All ER 344.
[30] *Esso Petroleum v Mardon* n 5.

Chapter 7

DURESS AND UNDUE INFLUENCE

This chapter covers duress and undue influence. A contract can be valid only if it is entered into freely. If one of the parties has been forced to enter into a contract through violence or a threat of violence, this amounts to duress, and this means that the contract is voidable. Similarly, if the plaintiff is unduly influenced into entering into a contract and this contract manifestly disadvantages them, this too renders the contract voidable.

1 DURESS TO THE PERSON

Threatening a person with physical harm or even death certainly amounts to duress. In *Barton v Armstrong*[1] Barton, the managing director of a certain company, was threatened with death by the defendant, its former chairman, if he did not agree to purchase the latter's shares in the company.

There was evidence to suggest that despite this threat, Barton was agreeable to the proposed purchase. The court held that this amounted to duress despite the fact that Barton might have entered into the contract anyway.

2 DURESS TO GOODS

The general rule in the past was that duress could not be applied to goods. The rigidity of this rule can be seen in *Skeate v Beale*.[2] In this case, a tenant only agreed to pay money he owed his landlords because the latter threatened to sell his goods immediately unless the agreement was made. The courts rejected the tenant's claim of duress to goods. However, if the defendant has no legal right to the goods, then the plaintiff is able to recover under duress. In *Maskell v Horner*,[3] the plaintiff was forced to pay toll money under a threat that if he did not pay, his market stall was to be closed and his goods seized. In fact, the tolls were demanded from him with no right of law whatsoever. The plaintiff was able to recover all his money.

[1] [1976] AC 104.
[2] (1840) 11 Ad & El 983.
[3] [1915] 3 KB 106.

The decision in *Skeate v Beale* was criticised by Kerr J in *Occidental Worldwide Investment Corp v Skibs A/S Avanti (The Sibeon and The Sibotre)*.[4] He stated:

> [I]f I should be compelled to sign a lease or some other contract for a nominal but legally sufficient consideration under an imminent threat of having my house burnt down or a valuable picture slashed through without any threat of physical violence to anyone, I do not think that the law would uphold the agreement . . . The true question is ultimately whether or not the agreement in question is to be regarded as having been concluded voluntarily.

This view was also endorsed in *The Atlantic Baron*,[5] and has been supported in other cases. In view of this fact, it might be safe to say that *Skeate v Beale* is no longer good law.

3 ECONOMIC DURESS

Economic duress occurs when a party has entered into a contract as a result of improper economic pressure. In such circumstances, they cannot be said to have entered into the contract freely. A classic example of this is where one party threatens to breach an existing contract unless the other party agrees to renegotiate its terms. In *Atlas Express Ltd v Kafco (Importers and Distributors) Ltd*,[6] Kafco had secured a large contract from Woolworths and obtained a hefty quantity of goods to fulfil it. Kafco contracted Atlas, a national road carrier, to distribute the goods to Woolworths' outlets.

Before entering into the contract, Atlas inspected the cartons for delivery. They estimated a minimum load of 400 cartons at a total cost of £440. However, when Kafco made its first load, there were only 200 cartons. This quantity, Atlas said, was not viable unless the full amount of £440 as per the estimated minimum load was paid. It was of utmost importance that Kafco be able to meet its delivery dates, as its commercial survival depended on it. Further, it would have been impossible to find alternative carriers to do so. Kafco thus agreed to the new terms, but later refused to pay at the new rate. The court held that Kafco was not bound by the new terms.

4 UNDUE INFLUENCE

A contract is also voidable where undue influence is found. It is difficult to give a precise definition of undue influence. As observed in *National Westminster Bank Plc v Morgan*[7] by Lord Scarman: 'there is no precisely

[4] [1976] 1 Lloyd's Rep 293.
[5] [1979] QB 705 per Mocatta J.
[6] [1989] QB 833.
[7] [1985] AC 686.

defined law setting limits to the equitable jurisdiction of a court to relieve against undue influence.' Further, in *Royal Bank of Scotland Plc v Etridge (No. 2)*,[8] it was observed that undue influence 'is something which can more easily be recognised when found than when exhaustively examined in the abstract'.

What is clear is that undue influence is based on some asymmetrical relationship of trust between the parties, which was then used to influence the weaker party to enter into an agreement. Such agreement must manifestly disadvantage the party claiming undue influence.[9]

In the case *Barclays Bank v O'Brien*,[10] the House of Lords examined the doctrine. This case concerned Mr O'Brien, who was a chartered accountant and director in a company in which he was an auditor. The company ran into financial troubles and the bank wished to find security for the company debts. Mr O'Brien offered the matrimonial home as security. He told his wife that the charge was limited to £60 000 and that it would only last for a few weeks.

Initially his wife refused but was later persuaded to sign, as her husband told her the company would fail if she did not. Further, she was told that her son, who had an interest in the company, would lose his home. Although the wife agreed to sign the charge, it turned out that the charge was not in fact limited in amount or in time.

The bank manager had sent the documents to their local branch with instructions that the wife be advised of the full extent of the liability. Further, he gave instructions that the wife should be advised to take independent advice before signing. However, the clerk simply got the wife to sign the documents without carrying out those instructions. When the bank sought to enforce the charge, the wife raised undue influence and misrepresentation in her defence to have the charge set aside.

Although she was successful with regard to misrepresentation, her defence in undue influence failed because she was held to exercise independence of thought on financial matters, and because she was used to dealing with the family finances.

In his judgment, Lord Browne-Wilkinson classified the categories of undue influence into two main categories. Class 1 is called 'actual undue influence'. Class 2, which is divided into two subcategories, Class 2(A) and Class 2(B), is called 'presumed undue influence'. These will be discussed in turn.

---

[8] [2002] 2 AC 773.

[9] See *BCCI v Aboody* [1989] 1 QB 923.

[10] [1993] 4 All ER 417.

Class 1: Actual undue influence

In order for someone to claim undue influence under Class 1, the plaintiff must prove affirmatively that the wrongdoer exerted undue influence for them to enter into a particular transaction.

Class 2: Presumed undue influence

In cases of presumed undue influence, the plaintiff only has to show that a relationship of trust and confidence between the complainant and the wrongdoer existed. This relationship should be of such a nature that it is fair to presume that the wrongdoer abused that relationship in persuading the complainant to enter into a transaction. These are divided into Class 2(A) and Class 2(B).

Class 2(A) relationships consist of certain relationships which, as a matter of law, raise the presumption that undue influence has been exercised. An example of such a relationship is that between an advocate and their client. It can also be the relationship between a doctor and a patient, or a pastor and a congregant. From the case of *Zambia Export and Import Bank Ltd v Mkuyu Farms*,[11] it would appear that the relationship between a banker and a customer in the course of business practice may not apply here.

Even if there is no relationship falling under Class 2(A), the complainant can still prove the de facto existence of a relationship 'under which the complainant generally reposed trust and confidence in the wrongdoer'. In such cases, we can say there exists a relationship which raises the presumption of undue influence. Under Class 2(B), therefore, the complainant can successfully set aside a transaction merely by proving that the complainant had trust and confidence in the wrongdoer.

[11] (1993–1994) ZR 36.

Chapter 8

MISTAKE

Mistake arises when one of the parties to a contact erroneously believes that certain facts are true at the time the parties are entering into it. At common law, mistake renders a contract void ab initio. This therefore means that no rights or obligations can arise under it. In equity, mistake renders a contract voidable. Therefore, rights and obligations will subsist until the contract has been avoided. In either scenario, the mistake must be an operative one.

1 COMMON MISTAKE

1.1 Res extincta

This applies to goods that have been in existence but have since perished. Section 6 of the Sale of Goods Act 1893 provides as follows: 'Where there is a contract for the sale of specific goods, and the goods without the knowledge of the seller have perished at the time when the contract is made, the contract is void.'

A leading case on *res extincta* is *Couturier v Hastie*,[1] where the plaintiff merchants had dispatched a consignment of corn. They thus sent the bill of lading to their London agent, who then hired the defendant to sell the corn. The defendant sold the corn on credit, unaware that the corn had fermented and become unfit for sale. The buyer repudiated the contract, on the ground that the goods did not exist. The plaintiffs sued the defendant, a del credere agent, to recover the purchase price. The court held that the action must fail because the contract presupposed that the goods were in existence when they were not. Cranworth LC stated:

> [T]he whole question turns upon the construction of the contract which was entered into between the parties . . . The contract plainly imports that there was something which was to be sold at the time of the contract, and something to be purchased. No such thing existing, I think the Court of Exchequer Chamber has come to the only reasonable conclusion upon it, and consequently that there must be judgment given by your Lordships for the Defendants in Error.

Further, in *Griffith v Brymer*,[2] the plaintiff made an oral contract at 11:00 to rent a room because he wanted to see the coronation procession. At this

[1] (1856) 5 HL Cas 673.
[2] (1903) 19 TLR 434.

point, none of the parties were aware that the coronation was postponed because of the King's illness. The court held that the contract was void based on mistake as to the fact.

Similarly, in *Galloway v Galloway*,[3] the court declared a deed of separation between a man and a woman null and void on account of the fact that it had been made under the mistaken assumption that the parties were married in the first place.

The High Court of Australia took a different approach in interpreting *Couturier v Hastie* in *McRae v The Commonwealth Disposals Commission*.[4] The plaintiffs in this case successfully made a bid to purchase an oil tanker from the defendants. This oil tanker, they were told, was situated on Journand Reef. Although the plaintiffs expended resources to find the tanker, they discovered that neither the tanker nor Journand Reef existed. The High Court awarded damages to the plaintiffs because the defendants had implicitly warranted the existence of the tanker. Although the situation was not fraudulently created, the defendants were careless and had no reason to believe that the tanker existed.

1.2 Res sua

When a person contracts to purchase an item that turns out to already belong to them, the contract will be void. This was illustrated in *Cooper v Phibbs*,[5] where Cooper had taken a lease from his uncle's daughter, Phibbs, of a fishery which Phibbs had inherited from her father. However, neither party was aware that Cooper already owned the fishery. The court held that the lease be set aside on the basis that there was a common mistake. Lord Westbury contended: 'If parties contract under a mutual mistake and misapprehension as to their relative and respective rights, the result is that that agreement is liable to be set aside as having proceeded upon a common mistake.'

1.3 Mistake as to quality

The case of *Bell v Lever Bros Ltd*[6] involved Bell and Snelling, who were chairman and vice-chairman of the Niger Company, a subsidiary of Lever Brothers. The two became redundant due to the amalgamation of the Niger Company with a third company, and Lever Brothers contracted to pay them

[3] (1914) 30 TLR 531.
[4] (1950) 84 CLR 377.
[5] (1867) LR 2 HL 149.
[6] [1931] All ER 1.

compensation, which was paid. It was later found out that they had committed breaches of duty which could have entitled Lever Brothers to dismiss them without compensation. Lever Brothers brought an action to recover the compensation paid. The House of Lords held that a mistake as to quality does render the contract void.

This was further affirmed in *Solle v Butcher*,[7] where Denning LJ held that mistake as to quality will never render a contract void at common law, no matter how fundamental that mistake is. He echoed this sentiment in *Leaf v International Galleries*,[8] where the plaintiff contracted with the defendants for the purchase of an oil painting of Salisbury described to him as a painting by Constable, a statement which was held to be part of the contract. It was later found that the painting was not a Constable and the plaintiff brought an action for the rescission of the contract. It was held that the plaintiff could not rescind the contract. Denning LJ opined:

> There was a mistake about the quality of the subject-matter, because both parties believed the picture to be a Constable; and that mistake was in one sense essential or fundamental. But such a mistake does not avoid the contract: there was no mistake at all about the subject-matter of the sale. It was a specific picture, 'Salisbury Cathedral.' The parties were agreed in the same terms on the same subject-matter, and that is sufficient to make a contract.[9]

In *Harrison & Jones Ltd v Lancaster Ltd*, the plaintiff and defendant entered into two contracts and agreed to the buying and selling of a quantity of Calcutta Kapok 'Sree' brand. It was later discovered that what the purchasers had in fact bought was not pure Kapok but contained a mixture of cotton, which was wholly unsuitable for the intended purpose. It was later established that both parties were of the view that Calcutta Kapok Sree brand was pure kapok. It was held that when goods are sold based on a known trade name or description without misrepresentation or breach of warranty, the fact that both parties are unaware that goods of that known trade description lack a particular quality is not relevant. The mistake in this case did not make the contract a nullity.

In essence, therefore, where parties are both mistaken as to the subject matter of their contract, neither can claim from the other for breach of contract. The parties are bound by their contract and, as such, the contract cannot be said to be a nullity on the ground of mutual mistake.

In *Grist v Bailey*,[10] a contract for the sale of a freehold property by the

[7] [1949] 2 All ER 1107.
[8] [1950] 1 All ER 693.
[9] See also *Harrison & Jones v Bunten & Lancaster* [1953] 1 All ER 903.
[10] [1967] Ch 532.

defendant to the plaintiff at a consideration of £850 was 'subject to the existing tenancy'. The defendant believed, and his agent assumed, that there was a protected tenant in occupation. The value of the property with vacant possession was £2 250 and, unknown to the defendant, the tenant and his spouse had died, and it was uncertain whether their son was entitled to protection. The plaintiff's claim was for specific performance, and the defendant counter-claimed for rescission on the grounds that the contract was void or voidable for mistake. The court held that a fundamental mistake existed, ie £850 against £2 250, and the defendant was not so at fault as to disentitle him to relief. The plaintiff's action was dismissed and the court ordered rescission.[11]

2 UNILATERAL MISTAKE

A unilateral mistake is said to exist where only one party is mistaken. This may be the case where one party is mistaken as to the identity of the other, or where one party intends to deal with one thing and the other party with another, or where there is a lack of ad idem on the terms of contract. Mistake as to the identity of the person or the subject matter is fundamental, but that alone does not void a contract. The cases of unilateral mistake may be categorised into mistakes as to the terms of the contract and mistakes as to identity, where the parties can be either *inter absentes* or *inter praesentes*.

2.1 Mistake as to the terms of the contract

Where one party is mistaken as to the nature of the contract and the other party is aware of the mistake, or the circumstances are such that they may be taken to be aware of it, the contract is void.

For the mistake to be operative, the mistake by one party must be as to the terms of the contract itself. In *Hartog v Colin & Shields*,[12] the defendants offered to sell 30 000 skins to the plaintiff at a certain price per pound. Previous negotiations had been carried on, as was a customary trade practice, by reference to price per piece. The value of a piece was about one third of the price per pound. The price was absurdly low, and the defendants claimed they had written 'pound' in error for 'piece'. The plaintiff's action for damages for breach of contract failed on the ground that the plaintiff could not have reasonably supposed that the offer contained the offerors' real intention.

[11] See *Laurent v Lexcourt Holdings Limited* [1978] 2 All ER 810.
[12] [1939] 3 All ER 566.

A mere error of judgement as to the quality of the subject matter will not suffice to render the contract void for unilateral mistake. In *Smith v Hughes*,[13] the plaintiff and the defendant entered into a contract for the sale of 40 or 50 quarters of oats by sample. The defendant agreed in writing that he would take the whole quantity at 34s a quarter. The plaintiff delivered a portion to the defendant, who complained that the oats were new. He thought he was purchasing old oats, new oats being of no use to him. The plaintiff, knowing his oats were new and having no old oats, refused to take them back and sued for the full price. There was variance in the evidence as to what transpired between the plaintiff and the defendant. It was held that the passive acquiescence of the seller in the self-deception of the buyer did not, in the absence of fraud or deceit on the part of the seller, entitle the buyer to avoid the contract, and that there must be a new trial.

Equity follows the law and will rescind a contract affected by unilateral mistake or refuse specific performance, as held in *Webster v Cecil*.[14] The defendant, having previously refused an offer of £2 000 to sell property to the plaintiff, wrote a letter offering to sell it for £1 250 as a result of a mistaken calculation. The plaintiff accepted this offer, but the defendant refused to honour the promise. A decree of specific performance was denied.

2.2 Mistake as to identity

The circumstances under which mistake as to the identity of a person may arise is usually in relation to the sale of goods, especially on credit: A seller is induced to sell to a buyer, believing that the buyer is one person or something else. Prior to paying for the goods, the buyer then sells them to a third party. When the seller discovers that the initial buyer is not who they purported to be, the seller has recourse against the third party. This type of mistake relates to the identity of the parties to the contract. The law makes a distinction between contracts where the parties are *inter absentes* and where the parties are *inter praesentes*.

2.2.1 *Contract made inter absentes*

Where the parties are not physically in each other's presence, eg they are dealing by correspondence, and one party is mistaken as to the identity not the attributes of the other, and intends instead to deal with some identifiable third party, and the other knows this, the contract will be void for mistake.

[13] (1871) LR 6 QB 597.
[14] (1861) 30 Beav 62.

This position was considered in the case of *Cundy v Lindsay*,[15] where a fraudulent person named Blenkarn, writing from 37 Wood Street, Cheapside, ordered goods in writing from Lindsay & Co, signing his name so it appeared like 'Blenkiron & Co'. A reputable firm known as Blenkiron & Sons which carried on business at 123 Wood Street was well known to Lindsay, who did not ascertain their correct address but dispatched the goods to 'Blenkiron & Co, 37 Wood Street, Cheapside'. Blenkarn, on receipt of the goods, sold them to the defendants. Lindsay brought an action in conversion, which succeeded. It was held that there was an operative mistake and no title passed to the defendants because no intention to contract with Blenkarn existed.

> [H]ow is it possible to imagine that . . . any a contract could have arisen between the claimants and Blenkarn, the dishonest man? . . . of him they knew nothing and of him they never thought. With him they never intended to deal. Their minds never, even for an instant time rested upon him, and as between him and them there was no consensus of mind which could lead to any agreement or any contract whatever.

If the innocent party believes that they are dealing with a reputable firm, not a rogue, then it would seem that the contract may be voidable for fraud but not void for mistake. This was held in *King's Norton Metal Co Ltd v Edridge Merrett Co Ltd*.[16] The plaintiffs, metal manufacturers at King's Norton, received a letter from Wallis, a fraudulent person, purporting to have been authored by a company known as 'Hallam & Co', Soho Hackle Pin and Fire Works, Sheffield, at the head of which was a representation that the company had offices in various cities. Wallis ordered goods from the plaintiffs on this headed paper and paid on a cheque signed 'Hallam & Co'. A second order was made on the same headed paper and the goods ordered were delivered. Wallis did not pay for these goods, and he sold them to the defendants. The plaintiffs brought an action against the defendants for the value of the goods, which failed. It was held that the contract was voidable for fraud but not void for mistake. The defendants acquired good title, because when title passed to them the contract had not yet been avoided. The plaintiffs could not show a confusion of entities for *Cundy v Lindsay* to apply.

In order to justify mistake as to identity, the following two elements must be present as highlighted in the above two cases: there must be an identifiable third party with whom one intended to contract; and the mistake must be as to identity, not attributes.

---

[15] (1878) 3 App Cas 459.
[16] (1897) TLR 98.

Cundy v Lindsay was recently confirmed by a majority of the House of Lords in *Shogun Finance Ltd v Hudson*.[17]

2.2.2 *Contract made inter praesentes*

Where the parties are *inter praesentes* (face to face), there is a presumption that the mistaken party intends to deal with the other person who is physically present and identifiable by sight and sound, irrespective of the identity which one or other may assume. For such a mistake to be an operative mistake and to make the agreement void, the mistaken party must show that:

(i) they intended to deal with someone else;
(ii) the party they dealt with knew of this intention;
(iii) they regarded identity as of crucial importance; and
(iv) they took reasonable steps to check the identity of the other person.

As such, even where the contract is not void, it may be voidable for fraudulent misrepresentation. But if the goods which are the subject matter have passed to an innocent third party before the contract is avoided, that third party may acquire a good title. This principle was highlighted in the case of *Phillips v Brooks*,[18] in which the plaintiff, a jeweller, commenced action against the defendants, who were pawn brokers, for the return of a ring (or, alternatively, its value) and damages for its detention. The defendants bought the ring from a fraudster called North, who walked into the plaintiff jeweller's shop and chose a ring and pearls valued together at £3 000. He produced a cheque book and, while signing it, represented that he was Sir George Bullough, and gave his address as St James' Square, London. The plaintiff checked the directory and found that Sir George lived at the named address. North took the ring. The cheque was dishonoured, but North had sold the ring to the defendants bona fide and without notice of the means by which he had acquired the ring. The court held that the plaintiff had intended to contract with North, and that good title had passed to the defendants.

The decision of the court is anchored in the fact that for mistake as to the identity of a person to suffice as sufficient to render a contract void, the party seeking to rely on the mistake must show that they did not intend to enter into a contract with the person in front of them. The overriding principle is that an error as to the person consequently annuls the contract

---

[17] [2003] UKHL 62.
[18] [1919] 2 KB 243.

only in circumstances where they are not present, and not when they are, as held in the above case.

In contrast, however, in the case of *Ingram v Little*[19] (a controversial case), a jointly owned car was advertised for sale by the three plaintiffs. A rogue introduced himself as Hutchinson and offered to buy the car. He offered to pay by cheque but one of the plaintiffs refused to accept it. The rogue then claimed to be PGM Hutchinson of Stanstead house. One of the plaintiffs checked the telephone directory and confirmed that there was a PGM Hutchinson at the named address. The plaintiffs then accepted the cheque and let the rogue have the car. The cheque was dishonoured but the rogue, who was not in fact Hutchinson, had sold the car to the defendant. The plaintiffs brought an action for return of the car and damages for conversion. The contract with the rogue was held to be void, and judgment was given for the plaintiffs.

The Court of Appeal held that the offer to sell on payment by cheque was made only to the person whom the swindler had represented himself to be, and, as the swindler knew this, the offer was not one which was capable of being accepted by him. Therefore, there had been no contract for the sale of the car by the plaintiffs and they were entitled to recover the car or damages from the defendant.

In *Lewis v Avery*,[20] the plaintiff advertised his car for sale. A rogue rang without giving a name and arranged to view the car. After test driving it the rogue decided to buy the car. The plaintiff agreed to sell his car to the rogue masquerading as Richard Green, a famous actor. On agreement of the price at £450, the rogue wrote out a cheque and signed it as RA Green and showed the plaintiff a studio pass with the name Richard Green and a picture of the rogue. The plaintiff was satisfied and let the fraudster keep the log book. The cheque was dishonoured but the rogue sold the car to the defendant, who bought in good faith. It was held that the plaintiff contracted effectively to sell the car to the rogue and could not therefore succeed against the defendant. The contract with the fraudster was voidable for fraud and not void for mistake. The contract had not been avoided when the sale was made to the defendant.

[19] [1960] 3 All ER 332.
[20] [1971] 3 All ER 907.

An exception to the above rule is that if a party intended to contract only with the person so identified, such a mistake will render the contract void. In *Lake v Simmons*,[21] the plaintiff brought an action to recover from his insurance company losses made in a transaction with a rogue. This case involved a woman who came to the plaintiff's shop and claimed to be the wife of Van der Borgh, and that her husband wished to buy her a necklace. The plaintiff, believing her, allowed her to take two necklaces to show her husband. The woman was in fact not Van der Borgh's wife. She sold the necklaces and kept the proceeds and was later convicted of larceny for the same. The insurance company argued that they were not liable to pay because the plaintiff caused the rogue to have possession of the necklaces. The court held that when the plaintiff let her take possession of the necklaces, there was no consensus ad idem between them and therefore the necklaces were not entrusted to her. Therefore, the plaintiff was entitled to recover from the insurance company.

3 MUTUAL MISTAKE

For any contract to be valid there must be consensus ad idem, or a meeting of minds, in relation to the subject matter of the contract. A mutual mistake is one where both parties fail to understand each other. This means that parties are at cross-purposes about each other's intentions. As a result of this no agreement is made because of the absence of offer and acceptance.

In cases where the parties misunderstand each other's intentions and are at cross-purposes, the court will apply an objective test. The courts thus consider what a 'reasonable man' would take the agreement to mean. If the test leads to the conclusion that the contract could be understood in one sense only, it means that both the parties will be bound in that sense.

However, if the transaction is totally ambiguous under this objective test, it means that there will be no consensus ad idem. In such cases the contract will be void.

In the case of *Wood v Scarth*,[22] the plaintiff, after an interview with the defendant's clerk, accepted an offer to rent a pub from the defendant at £63 per annum. It was the plaintiff's belief that the only payment to be made was £63. The defendant, on the other hand, intended that a premium of £500 be payable as well, a position which was never brought to the attention of the plaintiff by the defendant's clerk. The defendant refused to complete the transaction, and the plaintiff brought an action for specific

[21] [1927] AC 487.
[22] (1858) 1 F & F 293.

performance, which action failed. The plaintiff was, however, awarded damages.

Another good illustration is the case of *Scriven Bros v Hindley & Co.*[23] The case related to an action by the plaintiffs to recover the price of some Russian tow sold to the defendants by the plaintiffs at an auction. The defendants had made a bid at an auction to buy two lots, both having the same mark, and believed to contain hemp. Witnesses gave evidence to the effect that, in their experience, tow and hemp had never been landed from the same ship and under the same shipping mark. The defendants had been shown samples of hemp as being samples of what was contained in the shipping marks in question.

According to Lawrence J, the facts demonstrated that the parties were not ad idem, therefore the plaintiffs could recover only if the defendants were estopped from relying on what was now admittedly the truth. He held that the defendants were not estopped, since their mistake had been caused by or contributed to by the negligence of the plaintiffs.

If the contract is void at law on the ground of mistake, equity 'follows the law'. Specific performance will be refused and, in appropriate circumstances, the contract will be rescinded. However, even where the contract is valid at law, specific performance will be refused if to grant it would cause hardship. Thus the remedy of specific performance was refused in *Wood v Scarth*. This was based on the fact that for there to be a valid contract, the minds of the parties must meet. However, where mistake arises from mutual oversight from the parties and not from the negligence or intention of one of the parties, either party should be free from liability for any breach.

4 MISTAKE RELATING TO DOCUMENTS: *NON EST FACTUM*

Where a person appends their signature to a document, they are deemed to know what its contents are. As a general rule, therefore, a person is bound by their signature to a document, whether or not they have read or understood the document.[24] However, if fraud or misrepresentation has been used to induce a person to sign a contractual document, the transaction will be voidable.

Sometimes the plea of *non est factum*, namely that 'it is not my deed', may be available to a party to a contract executed by mistake. A successful plea makes a document void. The plea was originally used to protect illiterate and blind persons who were tricked into putting their mark on

[23] [1913] 3 KB 564.
[24] *L'Estrange v Graucob* [1934] 2 KB 394.

documents. It eventually became available to literate persons who had signed a document believing it to be something totally different from what it was.

For example, in *Foster v MacKinnon*[25] the plaintiff, as endorsee of a bill of exchange worth £3 000, sued the defendant, the alleged endorser of the same. The defendant, a man advanced in years, signed the bill of exchange, having only been shown the back of the document, after being told it was a guarantee similar to one he had signed previously. The court held in favour of the defendant. Byles J stated:

> It seems plain, on principle and on authority, that if a blind man, or a man who cannot read, or who, for some reason (not implying negligence) forbears to read, has a written contract falsely read over to him, the reader misreading it to such a degree that the written contract is of a nature altogether different from the contract pretended to be read from the paper which the blind or illiterate man afterwards signs; then at least if there be no negligence, the signature obtained is of no force. And it is invalid not merely on the ground of fraud, where fraud exists, but on the ground that the mind of the signer did not accompany the signature; in other words, he never intended to sign and therefore, in contemplation of law, never did sign the contract to which his name is appended. In the present case . . . he was deceived, not merely as to the legal effect, but as to the actual contents of the instrument.

The use of the rule in modern times has been restricted. For a successful plea of *non est factum*, two factors have to be established. First, it has to be established that the signer was not careless in signing. Secondly, it has to be shown that there is a radical difference between the document which was signed and what the signer thought they were signing.

The House of Lords decision of *Saunders v Anglia Building Society (Gallie v Lee)*[26] is the leading case on this topic. Mrs Gallie, a 78-year-old woman, signed a document which her nephew's friend, Lee, told her was a deed gifting the house to her nephew. She did not read the document, as she had broken her spectacles. The document was in fact a deed assignment assigning her leasehold to Lee. Lee mortgaged the interest in the house to a building society; on default, the building society brought an action for possession. Mrs Gallie sued for a declaration that the deed was void and for the recovery of the title deeds. When she died, the action was taken over by her executrix, Saunders.

The House of Lords held that the plea of *non est factum* can only rarely be established by a person of full capacity and that, although it is not confined to the blind and illiterate, any extension of the scope of the plea would be kept within narrow limits. In particular, it is unlikely that the plea

---

[25] (1868) LR 4 CP 704.
[26] [1970] 3 All ER 961.

would be available to a person who signed a document without informing themselves of its meaning.

The law of contract is premised on the fact that a party is deemed to have read and understood the contents of a document prior to signing it. They therefore cannot go back and claim mistake, fraud or misrepresentation.

The burden of establishing a plea of *non est factum* falls on the party seeking to disown the document. First, the person must show that in signing the document, they had acted with reasonable care. Carelessness on the part of the person signing the document would later preclude them from pleading *non est factum*. This is because no one should be allowed to take advantage of their own wrong. Secondly, one must show that there is a radical or fundamental distinction between the document as it is and the document as it was believed to be.

Chapter 9

VOID AND ILLEGAL CONTRACTS

A contract may have all the necessary ingredients, ie offer, acceptance, intention to create legal relations and capacity of the parties; but even where the elements above are satisfied, a contract will be rendered void if it is contrary to public policy or illegal. In sum, it is not possible to enforce a contract which involves a legal wrong.

1 VOID CONTRACTS

Void contracts can be classified into three main categories: those in restraint of trade, those to oust the jurisdiction of the courts and those prejudicial to the married state.

1.1 Contracts in restraint of trade

Contracts with the object of preventing or restricting business competition are regarded as void. In *Kores Manufacturing Co Ltd v Kolok Manufacturing Co Ltd*,[1] two manufacturers of carbon paper and typewriter ribbons agreed not to employ each other's former employees for a period of five years after they had left their original employer. Although the parties were entitled to protect their trade secrets, the court found that the agreement was invalid as it extended to all employees regardless of whether they knew the trade secret, and that the five-year period was too excessive. The claimants' chief chemist sought employment with the defendants, and the claimants were quite unwilling to consent to this. The claimants sought an injunction to enforce the agreement. The Court of Appeal refused to grant relief. Jenkins LJ opined:

> [I]t is true that the agreement of 1934 was between two employers and not between employer and employee, which was wholly and solely directed at preventing the employees of either contracting party, on ceasing to be employed by them, from entering employment of the other contracting party. It is not in doubt that employers are entitled to protect their interests by legitimate means ie by paying good wages and making their employment attractive. However an employer has no legitimate interest in preventing employees, after leaving employment from entering into the service of the competitor merely on grounds that the new employer is competitor.

[1] [1959] Ch 108.

In *Esso Petroleum Co Ltd v Harper's Garage (Stouport) Ltd*,[2] Harper owned and operated two garages, Mustow Green and Corner, and had entered into solus agreements with Esso Petroleum. In relation to Mustow Green, the agreement was to run for approximately four-and-a-half years, and it provided that Harper's Garage was to purchase only Esso Petroleum's oil, which would be supplied at a small discount. With regard to Corner, Esso Petroleum loaned Harper's Garage £7 000. The latter then mortgaged the garage premises for a period of 21 years. A contract containing a solus tie similar to that in the Mustow Green agreement was also entered into and was to last for 21 years. Harper's Garage began to sell petrol supplied by another company and the appellants sought to enforce the agreement. The House of Lords held that these agreements were in restraint of trade.

In *A Schroeder Music Publishing Co Ltd v MacCaulay*[3] MacCaulay, a young unknown songwriter, had entered into a publishing agreement with the appellant publishing company in which he assigned all copyright to the appellant for the whole world in each original composition and lyric for which he, whether solely or in collaboration, was responsible for the period of the agreement or at any time prior to it in so far as he still owned them. In addition, if the total royalties received during that term exceeded £5 000, the contract would be extended by a further five years. The publishers had the right to determine the agreement at any time by giving one month's notice. No such right had been given to MacCaulay. Further, the publishing company had the right to assign the agreement; the songwriter could not assign his rights under the agreement without obtaining the consent of the publisher. The publishing company was not under any obligation to publish any of MacCaulay's compositions. MacCaulay sought a declaration that the agreement was void because it was contrary to public policy. Lord Diplock opined:

> Because this can be classified as a contract in restraint of trade the restrictions that the respondent accepted fell within one of those limited categories of contractual promises in respect of which the courts still retain the power to relieve the promisor of his legal duty to fulfil them. . . . So I would hold that the question to be answered as respects a contract in restraint of trade of the kind with which this appeal is concerned is: was the bargain fair? The test of fairness is, no doubt, whether the restrictions are both reasonably necessary for the protection of the legitimate interests of the promisee and commensurate with the benefits secured to the promisor under the contract. For the purpose of this test all the provisions of the contract must be taken into consideration. My Lords, the provisions of the contract have already been sufficiently stated by my

[2] [1968] AC 269.
[3] [1974] 1 WLR 1308.

> noble and learned friend, Lord Reid. I agree with his analysis of them and with his conclusion that the contract is unenforceable.

From the common law it has thus been seen that contracts in restraint of trade are not enforceable. This is also the case under Zambian statutory law. Section 8(1) of the Competition and Consumer Protection Act 24 of 2010 provides as follows:

> Any category of agreement, decision or concerted practice which has as its object or effect, the prevention, restriction or distortion of competition to an appreciable extent in Zambia is anti-competitive and prohibited.

This also applies to vertical and horizontal agreements.[4] However, in the event that the vertical or horizontal agreements contain any provisions that are not prohibited, these provisions are severable and continue to have effect to the extent that they can be 'effected without the prohibited provisions'.[5]

1.2 Agreements to oust the jurisdiction of the courts

1.2.1 *Agreements for maintenance*

At common law a contract is said to be illegal if it purports to deprive or oust the jurisdiction of the court. For example, a clause in a contract to the effect that in an event of a dispute no recourse shall be had to the courts of law for enforcement of rights is illegal, as it is premised on ousting the court's jurisdiction which it would ordinarily have.[6] In *Hyman v Hyman*,[7] an agreement between a husband and wife following a divorce in which the husband promised to pay the wife an allowance in lieu of the wife applying to court for maintenance was held to be illegal.

1.2.2 *Arbitration clauses*

These are clauses in which parties to a contract agree to refer any dispute arising from the contract to arbitration before seeking recourse from the courts. In *Scot v Avery*,[8] a clause of this kind was upheld as it did not purport to oust the jurisdiction of the court, but simply to lay down the stages of dispute resolution.

1.3 Agreements prejudicial to the married state

There are various types of agreements which may arise under this type of contract, namely an agreement in restraint of marriage. This may, for

---

[4] See sections 9 and 10 of the Competition and Consumer Protection Act 24 of 2010.

[5] Ibid section 11.

[6] *Anctil v Manufacturers Life Insurance Company* (1899) AC 604.

[7] (1929) AC 601.

[8] (1855) 5 HLC 811.

example, take the form of a promise not to marry anyone but a specified person. The other form is a marriage brokerage contract whereby a person in consideration for money promises to procure the marriage of another person.[9]

2 ILLEGAL CONTRACTS

2.1 Agreements to commit an unlawful act

A contract is illegal if its execution is prohibited by law. For example, where A enters into a contract with B for the supply of narcotics, such contract is illegal, null and void and unenforceable. This means that no party thereto can enforce their rights under this contract because of the express prohibition by law. The nature of the illegality may take various forms which would inter alia include contract to commit a crime,[10] contract to commit a civil wrong,[11] unlawful method of performance,[12] contract to share proceeds of crime, to indemnify against liability for wrongful act,[13] etc.

In *Koufou v Greenberg*,[14] the plaintiff had entered into an illegal contract with the defendant. They had essentially agreed to convert £8 000 into K24 000. The plaintiff gave K24 000 to the defendant and the defendant wrote out a cheque which he sent to Greece. However, the defendant later sent instructions to his bankers not to cash that cheque. As a result of this transaction, the plaintiff was investigated by the Special Investigation Team for Economy and Trade (SITET) and was fined K13 512, which he paid. Because of this fine, the plaintiff brought an action. The court held:

> [T]he plaintiff's advocates must have known the principle ex turpi causa non oritur ratio. The plaintiff by entering into that bargain with the defendant was contravening the Exchange Control Act, Cap. 593. In other words, he had together with the defendant committed a crime against our laws of the land . . . The plaintiff committed a crime by exchanging our currency for the British sterling without the consent of the Minister of Finance as required by law. The agreement between the two was injurious to the public or against public good and as such this is invalidated on the grounds of public policy (see para. 392 op cit). The agreement was entered into for the purpose of evading the Exchange Control Act hence void ab initio and the plaintiff cannot reap from an illegal contract.

---

[9] *Goldsmith v Bruning* (1700) 1 Eq Ca Abr 89, pl 4.
[10] *Bostel Bros Ltd v Hurlock* [1949] 1 KB 74.
[11] *Allen v Rescous* (1676) 2 Lev 174.
[12] *Little v Poole* (1829) 9 B & C 192.
[13] *Cointat v Myheam & Sons* (1913) 2 KB 220.
[14] (1982) ZR 30 HC.

In *Mundanda v Mulwani And The Agricultural Finance Co Ltd and Mwiinga,*[15] the first respondent agreed in writing to sell part of his farm to the appellant, which was on mortgage to the second respondent for K20 000, regardless of whether that part of the farm was valued at a lesser amount by the Lands Department. The first respondent later offered the whole farm to the third respondent, and the K20 000 paid by the appellant was refunded to him by the second respondent. The appellant argued that damages were not an adequate remedy because he had already moved onto the land, and the third respondent had acted fraudulently. The first respondent argued that the agreement to pay K20 000, even if that was more than the valuation fixed in the Presidential consent, made the contract illegal and the contract could therefore not be enforced. The first respondent argued that he would face great hardship if specific performance was granted. Here the Supreme Court held that an illegal contract is capable of being performed legally.

2.2 Agreements prejudicial to the interest of the State

Examples of contracts prejudicial to the interest of the State would include trading with the enemy. A contract made during a war to which this country is a party is illegal if it relates to commercial transactions with the enemy. Such contracts are illegal as they tend to jeopardise the economy of this country and aid that of the enemy,[16] as are contracts relating to doing illegal acts in foreign friendly countries,[17] contracts relating to corruption, etc.

2.3 Contracts to promote sexual immorality

Any contract intended to promote sexual immorality is illegal and unenforceable. It is important, however, in modern contract law to draw a line between contracts with a meretricious purpose and those intended to regulate stable extra-marital relationships.

Meretriciously purposed contracts relate to a promise by a man to pay a woman money if she will become his mistress. This sort of contract is illegal.[18] On the other hand, a contract to pay someone with whom a promissor had illicitly cohabited in the past is not contrary to public policy since it does not promote immorality.

---

[15] (1987) ZR 29 (SC).
[16] *Sovfracht (V/O) v Van Udens Scheepvaart an Agentuur Maatschappij* (1943) AC 203.
[17] *Regazzoni v KC Sethia Ltd* (1958) AC 301.
[18] *Franco v Bolton* (1797) 3 Ves 368. Also *Benyon v Nettlefold* (1805) 3 Mac & G 94.

3 EFFECTS OF ILLEGALITY

3.1 On actions on the contract

In *Pearce and Another v Brooks*,[19] the plaintiffs entered into a contract to hire out a brougham (carriage) to a prostitute for the purposes of her profession. The plaintiffs were aware of the defendant's course of business. When the plaintiffs sued to recover the price of the brougham, the claim failed for illegality. This was based on the principle of *ex turpi causa non oritur actio*. Thus anyone supplying something for the performance of an illegal act with knowledge of it cannot sue for the price.

This can be contrasted with the decision in *Marles v Philip Trant & Sons Ltd MacKinnon and Third Party*,[20] where the defendants purchased wheat which they had thought was spring wheat called 'Fylgia'. However, the sellers had knowingly delivered another type of wheat called 'Vilmorin', which was a winter wheat. The defendants, in good faith, sold this wheat to the plaintiffs. This contract however did not comply with section 1 of the Seeds Act 1920, which required that an invoice giving certain information about seeds be furnished to a buyer, and was therefore illegal. The plaintiffs discovered that the wheat was winter wheat and as such sued the defendants. The Court of Appeal held that the plaintiffs, as the innocent party, could recover damages from the defendants. Further, since the defendants' statutory offence was one of inadvertence and no damage resulted from it, they were also entitled to recover from their suppliers the loss arising from the contract with the plaintiffs.

In *Strongman (1945) Ltd v Sincock*[21] the claimants, a firm involved in building, entered into a contract to modernise some property that belonged to the defendant, an architect. In order to do this work the defendant was required to have a licence without which it was illegal to do the work. Under the Defence (General) Regulations, as a condition precedent to being granted the contract, the defendant agreed to obtain the said licence, on the basis of which the contract was concluded. The claimants did work to the value of £6 359. However, licences to the value of only £2 150 had been obtained. The defendant agreed to pay the claimants £2 090 and refused to pay the balance on the grounds that the contract had been illegally performed. The claimants therefore sued and were successful in the Court of Appeal.

---

[19] (1966) LR 1 Ex 213.
[20] [1954] 1 QB 29.
[21] [1955] 2 QB 525.

In *Archbolds (Freightage) Ltd v S Spangett Ltd*,[22] the defendants contracted to carry a consignment of whisky belonging to a third party in a van which had no road licence, contrary to the Road and Rail Traffic Act, which made it an offence to carry goods in a goods vehicle without an 'A' licence. The claimants were not aware that the defendants did not have an 'A' licence. In carrying the whisky without the licence the defendants committed a statutory offence. The consignment of whisky was stolen during the journey. The defendants argued that because the contract was illegal it was therefore unenforceable. The Court of Appeal disagreed and found in favour of the claimants and held that they could recover damages for breach of contract.

Pearce LJ opined that the claimants had proved, as they ought to, that they had believed that the defendants could lawfully carry the goods in their van. The innocent party must succeed even though the illegality was statutory. Further, Devlin LJ opined: 'I think that the purpose of this statute is sufficiently served by the penalties prescribed for the offender; the avoidance of a contract would cause grave inconvenience and injury to members of the public without furthering the object of the statute.'

3.2 On actions for the recovery of property

There can be no recovery of property transferred under such a contract, and this was illustrated in *Taylor v Chester*.[23] In this case half of a £50 Bank of England note had been pledged as security from the expenses of a debauch in a brothel. The effect of the pledge was to transfer special property in the note to the pledgee, with the result that the pledgor would recover the note without tendering the amount due. The court held that the note could not be recovered. This was because the plaintiff could not recover it without revealing the true nature of the contract to which he himself was a party. Since the said contract was illegal, there could be no recovery.

In *Bowmakers Ltd v Barnet Instruments Ltd*,[24] the plaintiffs commenced action against the defendants for damages for conversion of certain machine tools, alleging that the tools belonged to them. The tools were transferred to the defendants subject to three hiring agreements between the plaintiffs and the defendants, each containing a purchase option. These contracts were illegal because they contravened wartime regulations. The defendants failed to keep up with the instalments and sold some of the tools

22 [1961] 1 QB 374.
23 (1869) LR 4 QB 309.
24 [1945] KB 65.

while refusing to return the rest to the plaintiffs. The plaintiffs sued under the tort of conversion because the goods belonged to them, and not on the basis of the illegal contracts. The defendants on the other hand contended that no action could be brought without the plaintiffs resorting to the illegal contracts. The Court of Appeal disagreed. Du Parcq LJ stated: 'we shall assume in favour of the defendants that the three hiring agreements were all, as they allege, and for the reasons which they give, affected by illegality.' Illegality in this case was with reference to the fact that the hiring agreements were subject to and in breach of wartime regulations.

In *Tinsley v Milligan*,[25] the dispute arose out of an agreement between a claimant and a defendant relating to a house in which they jointly lived as lovers and ran as a lodging house. The house was purchased from money contributed by both parties and, even though they had agreed that the house would be owned by them jointly, it was conveyed in the name of the claimant for purposes of enabling the defendant to make false claims for social security on the basis that she was not a property owner. The women eventually fell out and Tinsley brought an action for sole possession of the house. Milligan argued that the house was held in trust for both parties in equal shares. Tinsley contended that the house had been bought solely in her name and had been to further and illegal purpose. As such, in Tinsley's view, Milligan had no equitable rights under the transaction. The House of Lords found in favour of Milligan.

The court held that the claim would have been fortified by proof that the defendant had intended to make a gift; and if the claimant had proved this, then the defendant's claim to a share of the property would have failed.

3.3 Severance

In appropriate circumstances, an illegal or void part of a contract may be severed by taking out the objectionable part, enabling that which remains to be enforced. There are three main forms of severance: severance associated with dealing,[26] severance of an objectionable promise,[27] and severance of an objectionable part of the term of the contract.[28]

In the case of *Attwood v Lamont*,[29] the claimants had a general outfitters business at Kidderminister. It was divided into several departments, each of which was supervised by one of their employees. The head of each

[25] [1994] 1 AC 340.
[26] *Amoco Australia v Rocca Bros Motor Engineering Co* (1973) HCA 40; 133 CLR; 1 ALR 385.
[27] *Brooks v Burns Philp Trustee* (1969) HCA 4; 121 CLR 432; (1969) ALR 321.
[28] *Bacchus Marsh Concentrated Milk Co v Joseph Nathan & Co* (1919) HCA 18; 26 CLR 410.
[29] [1920] 3 KB 571.

department undertook that after leaving the service of the claimants they would not be concerned in any of the claimants' trade and business within 10 miles from the claimants' place of business. In action to enforce their rights against one of the heads of the departments, the claimants agreed that the radius of restraint was too wide in a point of subject matter, but argued that everything except reference to tailoring should be severed, and that part alone enforced. Young LJ opined:

> The doctrine of severance has not, I think gone further than to make it permissible in a case where the covenant is not really a single covenant but is in effect a combination of several distinct covenants. In that case and where severance can be carried out without the addition or alteration of a word, it is permissible. But in that case only.[30]

[30] See also *Ronbar Enterprises v Green* [1954] 1 WLR 815 and *Scorer v Seymour Jones* [1966] 1 WLR 1419.

Chapter 10

DISCHARGE OF CONTRACT

A contract may be discharged by performance, agreement, breach, or frustration. Once a contract is discharged, all rights and obligations of the parties are extinguished. The case of *Development Bank of Zambia v Mambo*[1] demonstrates the absolute nature of this rule. Mambo was employed by the Development Bank of Zambia (DBZ). On 6 November 1992, Mambo received a letter from the DBZ giving him three months' notice of termination of employment. This was to run from 6 November 1992.

Thereafter, Mambo was paid three months' salary in lieu of notice, which was based on his then-current salary. On 1 February 1993, the DBZ revised the salaries of its employees, including Mambo's category, which was backdated with effect from 1 November 1992. Mambo contended that since he did not receive his notice until 6 November 1992, this backdated increase should apply to him. Although the Supreme Court held that there was sufficient evidence that the letter of dismissal was only received on 6 November, '[s]uch a notice can never, at law, be backdated, and he is entitled to be paid from 1st November, up to and including 6th November, 1993, at the old rate payable under his then existing contract'.[2]

1 PERFORMANCE

1.1 The general rule

As a general rule, the parties must perform precisely all the terms of the contract, express and implied, in order to discharge their obligations.[3] In *Re Moore and Landauer*,[4] there was a contract for the sale of 3 000 tins of canned fruit. This was provided that the tins were packed in cases of 30 tins each. On delivery, the buyer discovered that about half the cases contained only 24 tins, although the contractual number of tins were delivered and the

[1] (1995–1997) ZR 89.

[2] Per Gardner JS.

[3] See also section 13 of the Sale of Goods Act, which says: 'Where there is a contract for the sale of goods by description, there is an implied condition that the goods shall correspond with the description; and if the sale be by sample, as well as by description, it is not sufficient that the bulk of the goods corresponds with the sample if the goods do not also correspond with the description.'

[4] [1921] 2 KB 519.

market value was unaffected. The buyer rejected the consignment. The Court of Appeal held that the buyer was entitled to reject this consignment. Not packing the tins was certainly a breach of the condition that goods must correspond with the description, as provided for in section 13 of the Sale of Goods Act 1893.

1.2 Exceptions to the general rule

1.2.1 *Divisible contracts*

A contract may be entire or divisible. An entire contract entails that complete performance by one party is a condition precedent to contractual liability on the part of the other party. On the other hand, a divisible contract means that part of the consideration of one party is set off against part of the performance by the other.

In *Sumpter v Hedges*,[5] the complainant had entered into an agreement under which he was to erect some buildings for the defendant for a sum of £565. He had done work worth £333 before he stopped building. The works were then completed by the defendant. The court held that the complainant was not entitled to recover for the partial work done. This was because he had abandoned the contract. This can be contrasted with *Roberts v Havelock*,[6] where a shipwright had entered into an agreement for the repair of a ship. The contract did not expressly state when payment was due. When he discontinued the works, the court held that he was not bound to complete the repairs before claiming some payment.

Treitel notes that whether a particular contract is entire or divisible really depends on the circumstances of the case. Where a party does agree to work under a contract, the courts are typically reluctant to construe the contract as to require complete performance before any payment becomes due.[7]

1.2.2 *Acceptance of partial performance*

Acceptance of partial performance can occur where a party performs part of the task that they are contracted to do. In such circumstances, the promisee is entitled to accept or reject the work. If the promisee accepts the work, they are under an obligation to pay a reasonable price for the benefit received. However, it must be possible to infer from the circumstances that there was a free agreement between the parties that payment should be made for the goods and services supplied.

[5] [1898] 1 QB 673.
[6] (1832) 3 B & Ad 404.
[7] GH Treitel *The Law of Contract* (2011)702.

In *Christy v Row*,[8] a ship freighted to Hamburg port was prevented 'by restraint of Princes' from doing so. The consignees directed that the delivery be thus effected at another port and accordingly accepted delivery. The court held that the consignees were liable, under a contract implied from their directions for an alternative route, to pay freight *pro rata itineris*.

1.2.3 *Completion of performance prevented by the promisee*

If it is the promisee that prevents the promissor from performing all their obligations, then the latter is entitled to recover a reasonable price for what they have in fact done on a *quantum meruit* basis. In *Planche v Colburn*,[9] the complainant had agreed to write a book for a series published by the defendants. He was to be paid £100 for this. After collecting the necessary materials and writing part of the book, the defendants abandoned the series. The complainant was entitled to claim on the original contract and on a *quantum meruit* basis. Tinal CJ opined:

> The plaintiff does not seek to recover the whole sum contracted for, but only a fair remuneration for that part of the article which he had prepared, and which was rendered useless by the discontinuance of the work in which it was to appear. The object of the defendants evidently was, to have a publication adapted to persons in the younger classes of society. The question you have to consider is, what degree of credit you give to the defence; which, it appears to me, must amount to this, or it amounts to nothing: that after the contract was broken, an entirely new arrangement was made, to furnish the matter for publication in a separate form. It seems, that in the month of November the plaintiff thought that the subject was one better suited for separate publication; but undoubtedly, up to that time, he had been preparing it for juvenile readers; and the form and size of the proposed new work were not settled on that occasion. It might be, that the plaintiff considered the subject-matter was better adapted for a separate publication, without admitting that the MS. and drawings already prepared were suited to such a publication. It will be for you to say, whether you think that this was a separate bargain, in which the plaintiff gave up the old contract altogether; for if you do, then you must find your verdict for the defendants. The question is, was the first agreement entirely abandoned with the consent of the plaintiff, and an entire new arrangement made between the parties? For only in such case can the verdict be for the defendants.

1.3 Substantial performance

In the event that a person performs the entire contract, but their performance has a few major defects, such person can be said to have substantially performed their promise. In such instances, one can recover the contract price, reduced to the extent of their breach of contract. In *Dakin v Lee*,[10] the defendants agreed to erect a house according to certain

[8] (1808) 1 Taunt 300.
[9] (1831) 8 Bing 14.
[10] [1916] 1 KB 566.

specifications. However, they failed to follow those specifications. Here the Court of Appeal held that the builders were entitled to the contract amount less the value of the defects.

This can be contrasted with *Bolton v Mahadeva*,[11] where the plaintiff contracted with the defendant to install central heating in the latter's house. This was to be for a lump sum of £560. The completed installations had defects, which cost a sum of £174 to rectify. The court held that the plaintiff was not entitled to recover owing to the fact that there was no substantial performance.

1.4 Tender of performance

A tender of performance is an offer by a person who has bound themselves to fulfil a contract to carry out their obligations. An illustrating case of how this works is in *Startup v M'Donald*.[12] The plaintiff here had contracted to deliver ten tons of oil to the defendant within the last fourteen days of March. Payment was due to be made in cash at the end of that period. Delivery was tendered at 20:30 on 31 March. The defendant refused to accept the oil at that late hour. The court held that the tender of the oil was equivalent to performance and that the plaintiff was entitled to recover damages for non-acceptance.

It is, however, worth noting section 29(4) of the Sale of Goods Act 1893. The said Act, passed subsequently to the preceding case, provides that delivery may be treated as ineffectual unless it is made at a reasonable hour. What constitutes a reasonable hour is a question of fact.

1.5 Stipulations as to time of performance

In the absence of a contrary intention, time is at common law regarded as being of the essence. Therefore, a party that does not perform on time cannot enforce the contract against the other party.[13]

2 AGREEMENT

What has been created by agreement may also be extinguished by agreement. Thus an agreement by the parties to extinguish their rights and obligations under an existing contract can itself be binding. This is provided that it is made under seal or supported by consideration.

---

[11] [1972] 1 WLR 1009.
[12] (1843) 6 M & G 593.
[13] Section 10(1) of the Sale of Goods Act 1893.

3 BREACH

Failure to perform the terms of a contract amounts to a breach. A breach which is serious enough gives the innocent party the option of treating a contract as discharged. A breach can be signified in two ways: by express words or conduct; or through breaking a condition in such a way that it amounts to a substantial failure of consideration.

Once the repudiation has been communicated to the innocent party, that party has a choice as to whether to accept the repudiation or not. A question that arises is whether silence or inaction can amount to acceptance of repudiation. This issue was explored in *Vitol SA v Norelf Ltd*,[14] where one party to a contract repudiated the contract, while the other party neither acted nor affirmed the repudiation. Lord Steyn opined:

> Where a party has repudiated a contract the aggrieved party has an election to accept the repudiation or affirm the contract . . . (2) an act of acceptance of a repudiation requires no particular form: a communication does not have to be couched in the language of acceptance. It is sufficient that the communication or conduct clearly and unequivocally conveys to the repudiating party that the aggrieved party is treating the contract as an end. (3) . . . the aggrieved party need not personally, or by an agent, notify the repudiating party of his election to treat the contract as at an end. It is sufficient that the fact of election comes to the repudiating party's attention, for example notification by an unauthorized broker or other intermediary may be sufficient.

The innocent party does not have to wait until the date fixed for performance before commencing an action. They may immediately treat the contract as at an end and sue for damages.[15]

Where no set date by which the contract must be performed has been stipulated, the contract must be performed within a reasonable time. This was established in *Rio Restaurant Bakery and Service Station v Long*.[16]

4 FRUSTRATION

A contract may also be discharged when it is frustrated. Frustration essentially occurs where a subsequent change of circumstances has either rendered it impossible to perform the contract or the contract itself has been deprived of its commercial purpose. This is normally because of an event that is outside the control of either party.

[14] [1996] AC 800.

[15] See *Hochster v De La Tour* (1853) 2 E & B 678.

[16] (1969) ZR 41.

4.1 Tests for frustration

There are two alternative tests for frustration. The first is the 'implied term' theory propounded in the case of *Taylor v Caldwell*.[17] Here Blackburn J stated:

> The principle seems to us to be that, in contracts in which the performance depends on the continued existence of a given person or thing, a condition is implied that the impossibility of performance arising from the perishing of the person or thing shall excuse the performance.

In other words, the contract is only tenable if the person or thing is in existence. Once it no longer exists, this will render the contract impossible to perform. Lord Loreburn explained in *FA Tamplin v Anglo-Mexican Petroleum*[18] that the court —

> can infer from the nature of the contract and the surrounding circumstances that a condition which was not expressed was a foundation on which the parties contracted . . . Were the altered conditions such that, had they thought of them, the parties would have taken their chance of them, or such that as sensible men they would have said 'if that happens of course, it is all over between us'.

The other test for frustration is called the 'radical change in the obligation' test. This was adopted in the case of *Davis Contractors v Fareham UDC*.[19] Here Lord Radcliffe stated:

> Frustration occurs whenever the law recognises that without the default of either party a contractual obligation has become incapable of being performed because the circumstances in which performance is called for would render a thing radically different from that which was undertaken by the contract. *Non haec in foedera veni*. It was not this that I promised to do.

In *National Carriers v Panalpina*,[20] Lord Wilberforce was reluctant to choose between the theories. He took the view that they merged one into the other and that the choice depends on 'what is most appropriate to the particular contract under consideration'.

4.2 Examples of frustration

4.2.1 *Destruction of the specific object essential for performance of the contract*

If the specific object essential for performance of the contract is destroyed, this frustrates the contract. An example of this is in *Taylor v Caldwell*,[21]

[17] (1863) 3 B & S 826.
[18] [1916] 2 AC 397.
[19] [1956] AC 696.
[20] [1981] AC 675.
[21] n 17.

where Caldwell had entered into a contract with Taylor under which the latter was to use the former's music hall for concerts. The hall was accidentally destroyed six days prior to the concerts' scheduled start date. Taylor thus brought an action against Caldwell for breach of contract. The court held that the action could not succeed because performance of the contract was rendered impossible by the destruction of the music hall.

4.2.2 *Personal incapacity*

Personal incapacity of one of the key parties may also render a contract frustrated. This was illustrated in *Condor v The Baron Knights*.[22] A drummer in a pop group whose contract provided that he work seven days a week fell ill. This meant that he could only work four days a week. Another drummer who could play seven days a week was hired in his stead. The court held that the contract of employment was frustrated in a commercial sense by the drummer's illness.

In the case of *Phillips v Alhambra Palace Co*,[23] a contract had been entered into between a firm of music hall proprietors and a troupe of performers. One of the partners in the firm died and it was argued that the contract had been frustrated as a result. The court held that the contract was not frustrated. It could still be enforced against the surviving partners because it was not of a personal nature. This can be contrasted with the case of *Graves v Cohen*,[24] where the court held that the death of a racehorse owner frustrated the contract with his employee, a jockey. This is because the relationship that subsisted between them was one of mutual confidence. That relationship ceased to exist on his death.

In *FC Shepherd v Jeromm*,[25] the Court of Appeal held that a custodial sentence imposed on an apprentice was sufficient to frustrate the contract of employment. This is because it rendered the performance of the contract radically different from that which the parties contemplated when they entered into the contract.

4.2.3 *The non-occurrence of a specified event*

The non-occurrence of a specified event may also deem the contract frustrated, depending on the facts. The case of *Krell v Henry*[26] involved a plaintiff who owned a room overlooking the proposed route for the

[22] [1966] 1 WLR 87.
[23] [1901] 1 QB 59.
[24] (1929) 46 TLR 121.
[25] [1986] 3 All ER 589.
[26] [1903] 2 KB 740.

coronation procession of King Edward VII, which he let to the defendant for the purpose of viewing the procession. The procession did not take off due to the King's illness and the plaintiff sued for payment. It was held that the cancellation of the procession discharged the parties of their obligations since it was no longer possible to attain the real aim of the agreement.

This can be contrasted with the case of *Herne Bay Steam Boat Co v Hutton*,[27] where the defendant had chartered a vessel from the plaintiff for the two days of King Edward VII's coronation festivities. Paying customers were to be taken to see the naval review by the King at Spithead, which is where the fleet was anchored. The written contract provided that the purpose of the charter was 'viewing the naval review for a day's cruise round the fleet'. Owing to the King's illness, the review was cancelled. However, the fleet remained anchored at Spithead. In this instance the court held that the contract was not frustrated. In this case, it was still possible to take fare-paying customers to see the fleet.

4.2.4 *Interference by the government*

Interference by government may also render a contract frustrated. In *Mumba v Zambia Fisheries and Fish Marketing Corporation Ltd*,[28] the plaintiff had sued the defendants for breach of contract as they had altered some of his conditions of service and had failed to fulfil others. The defendants contended that the contract had been frustrated owing to the fact that the Mwanakatwe Salaries Commission, followed by a government directive, had altered the plaintiff's terms of employment. The High Court held that the government directive did amount to a frustrating event.

4.2.5 *Illegality*

A contract may also become frustrated if it later becomes illegal. In the case of *Re Shipton, Anderson and Harrison Brothers,*[29] there was a contract for the supply of wheat lying in a warehouse. Before delivery was made and title transferred, in accordance with the terms of the contract, the wheat was requisitioned by the government. This was in accordance with wartime emergency food control measures. The court held that the contract was discharged, as performance was made impossible by the requisition.

---

[27] [1903] 2 KB 683.
[28] (1980) ZR 135.
[29] [1915] 3 KB 676.

4.2.6 *Delay*

In *Jackson v Union Marine Insurance*,[30] the court held that a delay in repairs amounted to a frustrating event.

4.3 Limitations of the doctrine

The doctrine of frustration is applied in limited circumstances. As Viscount Simmonds stated in *Tsakiroglou v Noblee Thorl*,[31] 'the doctrine of frustration must be applied within very narrow limits'. Further, in *Pioneer Shipping v BTP Tioxide*,[32] Lord Roskill said that the doctrine of frustration was 'not lightly to be invoked to relieve contracting parties of the normal consequences of imprudent commercial bargains'.

4.3.1 *Express provision for frustration*

If there is an express contractual provision covering the frustrating event, the doctrine of frustration will not apply.

4.3.2 *Mere increase in expense or loss of profit*

A mere increase in price will not give rise to frustration. In *Davis Contractors v Fareham UDC*,[33] the plaintiffs contracted to build 78 houses for the defendant at a specified price. For various reasons, chief of which was the lack of skilled labour, the work took 22 months to complete and cost £17 000 more than anticipated. The plaintiffs argued that they were entitled to the £17 000 on a *quantum meruit* basis. This was because the contract had been frustrated by the lack of skilled labour. The court held that making the contract more difficult to perform by the unforeseen circumstances did not frustrate it.

Similarly, the case of *Tsakiroglou v Noblee Thorl*[34] involved a contract in which Tsakiroglou was to sell Sudanese groundnuts to Noblee Thorl. They were to be brought from Sudan to Hamburg in the November/December period of 1956. As a result of the Suez crisis, the Suez Canal was closed between 2 November 1956 and April 1957. Tsakiroglou failed to deliver, arguing that the only alternative route was through the Cape of Africa, which was commercially and fundamentally different. The court held that the contract was not frustrated. It was simply going to be more expensive or onerous to perform, but the change of circumstances was not fundamental.

[30] (1873) LR 10 CP 125.
[31] [1961] 2 All ER 179.
[32] [1982] AC 724.
[33] [1956] AC 696.
[34] n 31.

4.3.3 *Frustration must not be self-induced*

The frustration event should also not be self-induced. In *Maritime National Fish v Ocean Trawlers*,[35] the appellants chartered a steam trawler from the respondents which was fitted with an otter trawl. On renewal of the charter party, it was known to both parties that it was not legal to operate an otter trawl without a licence from the minister. The appellants operated five trawlers, including that owned by the respondents, and were granted three licences by the minister, giving them the right to choose which steamers got the licences. The appellants deliberately left out the respondents' trawler when assigning the licences and claimed that the lack of a licence frustrated the contract. The court held that there was no frustration of the contract, because the ostensible frustrating event was self-induced.

4.3.4 *Foreseeability of the frustrating event*

If the frustrating event is foreseeable, then frustration cannot be relied on. In *Walton Harvey Ltd v Walker & Homfrays Ltd*,[36] the defendants had entered into a contract with the plaintiffs in which the plaintiffs were to advertise on the defendants' hotel for seven years. Before the expiry of this period, the hotel was compulsorily acquired by a statutory order and demolished. The defendants claimed that the acquisition had frustrated the contract. The court held that the defendants were liable to pay damages because they knew of the risk of compulsory acquisition, which they could have prevented, while the plaintiffs did not.

4.4 Effects of frustration

The effects of frustration are covered in the Law Reform (Frustrated Contracts) Act, Chapter 73 of the Laws of Zambia. Section 3(2) provides three rules. The first is that money paid before the frustrating event is recoverable. Money payable before the frustrating event ceases to be payable, even where there has been a total failure of consideration. However, if the party to whom such sums are paid or payable incurred expenses before discharge on performance of the contract, the court may award them expenses up to the limit of the money paid or payable before the frustrating event.

---

[35] [1935] AC 524.

[36] [1931] 1 Ch 274.

Chapter 11

REMEDIES FOR BREACH OF CONTRACT

1 DAMAGES

1.1 Purpose of damages

The purpose of damages is to compensate the injured party for any consequences of the breach of contract. In other words, the courts are trying to put the injured party in the position that they would have been but for the breach of contract. Damages, however, should not be used as a means of punishing the defendant, as was pointed out in *Addis v Gramophone Co Ltd.*[1] Lord Atkinson opined: 'I have always understood that damages for breach of contract were in the nature of compensation, not punishment.'

1.2 Heads of damage and calculation

1.2.1 *Loss of bargain*

When we talk of loss of bargain, essentially we are saying that the injured party should be compensated for what they were expected to gain, had the breach not taken place and had the contract been properly performed.

In the case of *Gondwe v Supa Baking Company Ltd (In Liquidation) and Akubat*,[2] the defendant had promised to sell half of a semi-detached house to the plaintiff, which the latter had occupied as an employee. Neither the plaintiff nor the defendant were aware that the house had been sold as a whole by the agents to the Zambia Privatisation Agency a year previously. The Supreme Court held that, rather than disturbing the successive contracts, they would award damages to the plaintiff for breach of contract 'on the footing of damages for loss of bargain'.

1.2.2 *Reliance loss*

The courts can award damages if the claimant has incurred expenses in reliance of a contract which then becomes aborted. In *Anglia Television v Reed*,[3] for example, the plaintiffs had hired an actor, Robert Reed, to star in a movie. They had spent roughly £2 750 in finding a place to film it, a suitable actor and a suitable director.

[1] [1909] AC 488.
[2] SCZ Judgment 9 of 2001.
[3] [1972] 1 QB 60.

The actor had in fact double-booked, and could not fulfil his obligations under this contract. The plaintiffs failed to find a replacement and aborted the contract. The plaintiffs were able to sue for wasted expenditure. Lord Denning MR stated that one can claim not only for expenses incurred prior to the conclusion of the contract but also subsequently.

1.2.3 *Restitutionary interest*

Where a bargain is made and the price paid, the plaintiff is entitled to recover the price paid plus interest in the event that the defendant fails to deliver the goods bargained for.[4]

1.2.4 *Time for assessment of loss*

As a general rule, damages should be assessed at the time of the breach. However, as the case of *Johnson v Agnew*[5] illustrates, the courts can postpone the date for assessment of damages to a time which is more appropriate.

1.2.5 *Where the parties had the option to terminate*

Where the parties had an option to terminate, the courts are reluctant to allow a plaintiff to recover for 'virtually an indefinite period'. This was established in *Mobil Oil Zambia Ltd v Ramesh Patel.*[6] Ngulube DCJ (as he then was) opined:

> [I]t seems obvious to us that the defendant should not have been allowed to recover loss of profits in respect of the breach by the plaintiff, for what was virtually an indefinite period. The defendant had calculated his loss of profits, by the month, from October 1984, when deliveries of fuel stopped, right down to 11 March 1986, when he gave evidence in the witness box. This is clearly an unacceptable way of compensating a party for loss of profits as a result of the deliberate refusal, of which he was aware, by the other party to perform his part of the contract. The renunciation of the contract by the plaintiff in effect resulted in its wrongful termination. Where, as here, the contract-breaker had a contractual option to terminate the contract, the Court should assess the damages on the footing that the party in breach would have exercised the option . . . Indeed, this is frequently done in employment cases and the principle is equally applicable to the facts of this case. In our considered view, therefore, the damages for breach of contract, in terms of loss of profit for non-supply of fuel, should be limited to a period of one month, such being the period of notice to terminate specified in the contract.

---

[4] See *Millar's Machinery Co v David Way* (1935) 40 Com Cas 204.
[5] [1980] 1 All ER 883.
[6] (1988–1989) ZR 12.

1.3 Damages which are irrecoverable

Although the plaintiff is able to recover damages for injury to feelings in tort scenarios, such damages are not under the law of contracts. An illustrative case is that of *Addis v Gramophone Company*.[7] The contract in this case provided for six months' notice before termination of employment. Although this notice had been granted by the defendant company, they had prevented the plaintiff from doing his job. At first instance, damages were awarded for wrongful dismissal, including a sum that reflected the harsh and humiliating manner in which the plaintiff had been dismissed. However, on appeal, the House of Lords held that such damages were not recoverable and that the plaintiff's damages extended only to economic losses arising from the breach of contract.[8]

1.4 Other types of damage

1.4.1 *Discomfort, vexation and disappointment*

Damages may be awarded for discomfort, vexation and disappointment. Thus in *Jarvis v Swan Tours*,[9] the court held that the plaintiff could recover damages for the disappointment and discomfort he had been caused because the hotels and buses fell short of the standards promised by the defendant. However, these damages are limited only to instances 'where the contract which has been broken was itself a contract to provide peace of mind or freedom from distress'.[10]

1.4.2 *Inconvenience*

In addition, damages are also available in the event that the claimant has been inconvenienced. In *Bailey v Bullock*,[11] the claimant had to live with his wife's parents for a period of two years. This was a direct consequence of his solicitor failing to take proceedings to recover his house. The court held that the solicitor was liable for damages for inconvenience caused to his client.

---

[7] n 1.

[8] This position was reaffirmed in *Bliss v South East Thames Regional Health Authority* [1985] IRLR 308.

[9] [1973] 2 QB 233.

[10] Per Dillon LJ in *Bliss v South East Thames Regional Health Authority* n 8. The case of *Alexander v Rolls Royce Motor Cars* [1995] TLR 254 illustrates that the courts are quite unprepared to extend the instances in which damages for distress or disappointment may be awarded.

[11] [1950] 2 All ER 1167.

1.4.3 *Diminution of future prospects*

In *Dunk v George Waller*,[12] an apprentice was wrongfully dismissed. If he had been allowed to complete his apprenticeship, the apprentice would have obtained a certificate. In turn, the certificate would have entitled him to certain jobs at certain wages. These chances were diminished without this certificate. The court held that he was entitled to damages because the point of undertaking the apprenticeship was to enable him to get a better-paying job.[13]

1.5 Causation

There must be a direct causal link between the breach and the loss.[14] In the event that there are two factors contributing to the damage and both causes have equal effect, just one will be sufficient to bring about a claim for damages. This was illustrated in *Smith, Hogg & Co v Black Sea Insurance*,[15] where the cargo that a shipowner was carrying was damaged as a result of perils at sea as well as the general unseaworthiness of a ship. The court held that the fact that the ship was not seaworthy was sufficient to bring an action for damages.

Intervening acts of third parties do not necessarily absolve the defendant of liability if the intervening act was reasonably foreseeable. In *Stansbie v Troman*,[16] a painter had completed his work and then left the house in which he had been working unlocked. This house was later burgled by thieves. The court held that the defendant was liable for the value of the goods taken, as he should have foreseen this sort of loss and accordingly guarded against it.

Weld-Blundell v Stephens[17] is a contrasting case. Here, the plaintiff had engaged the services of the defendant, an accountant, to investigate a company that the former had invested in. The defendant's partner had negligently dropped a letter from the plaintiff in the office of the company manager. The company manager then picked it up and showed it to his directors, who then sued the plaintiff for libel and won. The plaintiff sued the defendant for breach of contract in order to recover the damages that he had to pay out in the libel action. The court dismissed the claim. This was because the plaintiff's liability for libel existed independently of the

[12] [1970] 2 QB 163.
[13] See also the case of *Chaplin v Hicks* [1911] 2 KB 786 for speculative damages.
[14] *Monarch Steamship Co Ltd v A/B Karlshamns Oljefabriker* [1949] AC 196.
[15] [1940] AC 997.
[16] [1948] 2 KB 48.
[17] [1920] AC 956.

contract. In addition to this, the loss was caused not by breach of contract but as a result of the company's manager showing the letter to his directors, an act which in their view could not have been foreseen by the defendant.

1.6 Remoteness of damage

The loss flowing from the breach must not be too remote. That is to say, losses recovered must be within the reasonable contemplation of the parties. In *Hadley v Baxendale*,[18] the claimants were millers in Gloucester. Their mill shaft had broken, and they had contracted with the defendant to repair it in Greenwich. It was supposed to arrive within a week; however, the defendant delayed and the claimants sued. It was held that the damages in this case were too remote. This case established two heads under which damages are recoverable: damages which may be fairly and reasonably considered as naturally arising from the breach; and damages which reasonably should have been in the contemplation of the parties as likely to result from the breach at the time that they contracted.

Thus, in the case of *Zambia Consolidated Copper Mines v Goodward Enterprises*,[19] the Supreme Court declined to uphold a claim for losses that were not within the knowledge and contemplation of the parties.

In *Victoria Laundry v Newman Industries*,[20] the defendants had delayed the delivery of a boiler for five months. The claimants sought damages for loss of the following profits: £16 per week which would have been earned in extra profits garnered from a new and improved boiler; and £262 per week which would have been earned from Ministry of Supplies from a lucrative contract.

The court held that the defendants were not liable for the second item because it was too remote. The defendants were not aware of the lucrative contract between the Ministry and the claimants.

This can be contrasted with *The Heron II*.[21] Because they had diverted, the defendant shipowners arrived at a destination nine days later than they were originally supposed to with a shipment of sugar. The plaintiffs had intended to sell the sugar immediately. By the time it arrived, however, the price of sugar had dropped. As a result, the plaintiffs sued for the loss of £4 000. This action succeeded. The court held that the defendant should have reasonably contemplated that the plaintiffs wished to sell their sugar immediately.

[18] (1849) 9 Exch 341.
[19] SCZ Judgment 7 of 2000.
[20] [1949] 2 KB 528.
[21] [1969] 1 AC 350.

1.7 Mitigation of loss

Once a breach has taken place, it is incumbent on the injured party to take reasonable steps to mitigate the loss caused by the breach of contract. In *Payzu v Saunders*,[22] the claimants sent a cheque to the defendants after receiving a delivery of silk. However, this cheque did not arrive. The claimants thus sent another cheque. Because of this, the defendants erroneously believed that the claimants were suffering financial difficulties. They therefore informed the claimants that they would not be delivering any more goods unless they paid in cash. The claimants refused to accept this and sued for breach of contract, claiming the difference between the contract and the market price.

The Court of Appeal refused to award damages for the difference in price. This was because the loss arose not from the breach of contract but from the claimants' refusal to accept the defendants' offer.

Further, a plaintiff is not expected to take risks in order to mitigate losses created by the defendant's breach of contract. This is illustrated in *Pilkington v Wood*,[23] where a solicitor had failed to inform the plaintiff that the property he was buying had a defective title. Harman J rejected an argument that the plaintiff should have mitigated his loss by suing the vendor. The judge said that 'it is no part of the claimant's duty to embark on the proposed litigation in order to protect his solicitor from the consequences of his own carelessness'.

Moreover, any benefits obtained by the plaintiff as a result of their mitigation must also be taken into account by the courts. This was established in the case of *British Westinghouse v Underground Electric Railway of London*.[24]

1.8 Liquidated damages and penalty clauses

Liquidated damages clauses effectively make a genuine assessment of the losses which are likely to occur as a result of a breach of contract. They will generally stipulate what sum is payable in the event of a breach. Another type of clause is the penalty clause, which is intended as a punishment for the person breaching the contract. Penalty clauses are void and are disregarded in actions for breach of contract. What is not as clear is how to determine whether a clause is a penalty clause or a liquidated damages clause.

---

[22] [1919] 2 KB 581.
[23] [1953] Ch 770.
[24] [1912] AC 673.

In *Dunlop Pneumatic Tyre Co v New Garage & Motor Co Ltd*,[25] the claimants had supplied tyres to the defendants. According to an agreement, the defendants were not to, inter alia, resell the tyres below the list price. If they did so, they would have to pay a sum of £5 'by way of liquidated damages and not as a penalty'. The House of Lords held that this was not a penalty clause but a limited damages clause. Lord Dunedin laid down various tests:

(1) If the sum stipulated is 'extravagant and unconscionable' in relation to the greatest conceivable loss that could follow the breach, then it will be held to be a penalty.
(2) Where breach consists of the non-payment of a sum of money and the sum payable upon breach is greater than the sum which was meant to be paid, then this is penalty.
(3) In the event that a lump sum is payable on the occurrence of one, or more or perhaps several events, some harmful and some not so harmful, then the lump sum is presumed (but no more) to be a penalty.
(4) However, a sum is not prevented from being liquidated damages merely by the fact that precise pre-estimation of the loss is impossible.[26]

2 SPECIFIC PERFORMANCE

The courts may also issue an order for specific performance. In such an event, the addressee is compelled by the court to fulfil the terms of the contract. These terms must be positive in nature. That is to say, they compel the party in breach to do something. This can be contrasted with injunctions, which are negative in nature. In other words, they prevent the party in breach from doing something.

Failure to comply with an order for specific performance may render the contract-breaker liable for proceedings for contempt of court. There are limits to when the court may grant an order for specific performance. Certainly if damages are an adequate remedy then, as a general rule, an order for specific performance will not be granted. The judiciary may also use their discretion. Further, we need to look at the type of contract.

2.1 Damages an adequate remedy

Specific performance will not be granted where damages are an adequate remedy. This was certainly the position taken in *Mobil Oil (Zambia) Ltd v Loto Petroleum Distributors Ltd*.[27] Hadden J opined:

[25] [1915] AC 79.
[26] See also *Cellulose Acetate v Widnes Foundries* [1933] AC 20, which seems to suggest that the amount payable is limited to the amount stipulated in the liquidated damages clause. This is the case regardless of the fact that possible damages have been underestimated.
[27] (1977) ZR 336.

> The court will not grant a decree of specific performance of a contract if the party seeking the decree can obtain a sufficient remedy by a judgment for damages and such a decree will not be made where it would be impracticable to secure compliance with it; 'The equitable principle of refusing specific performance extends to contracts involving personal service even though they are not contracts of service' (Chitty on Contracts, 23rd ed. Vol. I, paragraph 1529). For these reasons I do not consider it would be proper for the court to grant a decree of specific performance but an award of damages in favour of the defendant should be made instead.

However, damages may be inadequate in instances where the plaintiff cannot get a satisfactory substitute.[28] This is certainly provided for in section 52 of the Sale of Goods Act 1893, which states: 'In any action for breach of contract to deliver specific or ascertained goods the court may, if it thinks fit, on the application of the plaintiff, by its judgment or decree direct that the contract shall be performed specifically.' Damages will also be inadequate if the award of damages may be unfair to the plaintiff.[29] Further, damages will be inadequate where the amount payable is difficult to quantify. The courts can also exercise their discretion when making an order for specific performance where the situation calls for it.[30]

2.2 Type of contract

The courts will also look at the type of contract. The general rule is that the courts will not order specific performance on contracts involving personal service and building contracts.[31] This is because damages will be adequate to enable the injured party to acquire the services of another builder, for example.

3 INJUNCTION

The courts may also prevent the offending party from committing a breach by way of injunction. There are three types of injunction. One is an interlocutory or interim injunction. This is available to the plaintiff if they wish to regulate the position of the defendant pending a hearing. One may also obtain a prohibitory injunction. This type of injunction prevents the defendant from conducting themselves in a way that will breach the contract. Finally, a mandatory injunction is also available. This requires a defendant to reverse the effects of an existing breach.

[28] See generally *Nutbrown v Thornton* (1804) 10 Ves 159, *Cohen v Roche* [1927] 1 KB 169.

[29] *Beswick v Beswick* [1968] AC 58.

[30] See *Mundanda v Mulwani & Others* (1987) ZR 29 (SC) and *Zambia Bata Shoe Company v Vis-Mas Ltd* (1994) SJ 35 (SC).

[31] See the case of *Wolverhampton Corp v Emmons* [1901] 1 KB 515 for an exception.

4 DAMAGES IN LIEU OR IN ADDITION

Damages may of course be awarded in lieu of performance. However, they may also be awarded in addition to specific performance. An illustrating case is *Grant v Dawkins*.[32] The vendor in this case had a title to land which was subject to an encumbrance. This amounted to a breach of contract. The court held that the plaintiff could get specific performance of what title the defendant had; and, in addition to this, the plaintiff was entitled to damages based on the cost of discharging the encumbrance.

[32] [1973] 1 WLR 1406.

www.ingramcontent.com/pod-product-compliance
Ingram Content Group UK Ltd.
Pitfield, Milton Keynes, MK11 3LW, UK
UKHW051206260726
13967UKWH00011B/3134

9 781485 127574